Jennifer Paterson's
Seasonal Receipts

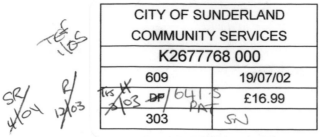
These recipes have previously appeared in the *Spectator*

'Artichoke Terrine with Cream and Chive Sauce' is reprinted by permission of
Pavilion Books from *Bouquet de Provence* by Jean Andre Charial
'Poulet Béarnais' is reprinted by permission of Chatto and Windus from
The Real Meat Cookbook by Frances Bissell
'Vegetables with Herb Cream' and 'Soft Meringues with Egg Custard' are extracted
from *European Festival Food* published by Bantam, a division of Transworld Publishers Ltd.
© Elisabeth Luard 1990. All rights reserved.
'Potatoes and Black Olives' is reprinted by permission of Rosendale Press from
Vegetable Market Cookbook by Robert Budwig
'Duck Liver Pâté with Orange Relish' is reproduced by permission of Thane Prince
'Amaretti and Strawberry Terrine' is reproduced by permission of Sophie Grigson
'Chilled Tomato Soup with Frozen Extra Virgin Olive Oil' is reproduced by permission
of Antony Worrall Thompson
'Watercress Mousse with Red Pepper Sauce' is reprinted by permission
of St John Ambulance from *Lincolnshire Cookery Book*
'Céleri Rémoulade' is taken from *Secrets of French Home Cooking* by
Marie-Pierre Moine (Conran Octopus)

First published in 1998
by HEADLINE BOOK PUBLISHING

10 9 8 7 6 5 4 3 2 1

British Library Cataloguing in Publication Data

Paterson, Jennifer
Seasonal receipts
1. Cookery
I. Title
641.5

ISBN 0 7472 2193 6

Photographer: Steven Lee   Home Economist: Wendy Lee
Stylist: Marian Price   Designer: Peter Ward

Typeset by Letterpart Ltd, Reigate, Surrey
Printed and bound in Italy by
Canale & C.S.p.A

HEADLINE BOOK PUBLISHING
A division of Hodder Headline PLC
338 Euston Road
London NW1 3BH

To my beloved director Patricia Llewellyn for my new life
and to Charles Moore who started me off on this lark

Also by Jennifer Paterson

Feast Days

Two Fat Ladies
(with Clarissa Dickson Wright)

Two Fat Ladies Ride Again
(with Clarissa Dickson Wright)

Jennifer's Diary:
A Diary of One Fat Lady

Jennifer Paterson's
Seasonal Receipts

HEADLINE

Contents

Introduction 9

Introduction

These receipts from my articles in the *Spectator* are the continuation of my first collection, published as *Feast Days*, which went up to 1990. In this new book, the publishers have grouped the receipts seasonally so that you can happily find something just right for the weather – even the summer heat which I so dislike. This arrangement prompted Headline to consider taking out my beloved Saints and their strange goings-on, but I know my readers love them as much as I do so lots of them have found their way back in. You can still contemplate as you cook.

Since entering the strange world of television fame, I don't have as much time for inventive cooking as I used to, so I am very grateful to all friends who produce new ideas for me and most heartfully thank all the people mentioned in this book who have passed on receipts to me; kisses all round.

Finally, I beg you to enjoy cooking. It is one of the few things you can only get better at which gives enormous satisfaction to yourself and to your beloveds. Hope this book will give you some fun, more feast days and zest for life. Toodle-pip.

Jennifer Paterson

Spring

SPRING

• • • • • • • • • • • • starters • • • • • • • • • • • •

Artichoke terrine with cream and
chive sauce
Crab au gratin
The Milford salad
Maccheroncini with mussels

La Ribollita
Asparagus and smoked salmon tarts
Chilled tomato soup with frozen extra
virgin olive oil

• • • • • • • • • main courses • • • • • • • • •

Coq au Riesling
Lamb stew with flageolet beans
Ragout of Lamb
Turkey loaf
Trout cooked in leeks
Oxtail with prunes

Steamed chicken
Fillet à la Meerlust with potato salad
Sea bass with black olives
Fish with spring vegetables
Feijoda

• • • • • • • accompaniments • • • • • • •

Creamy mushroom and potato gratin
Scottish nettle pudding
Banana raita

Vegetables with herb cream
Potatoes and black olives
Banana and bacon rolls

• • • • • • • • • desserts • • • • • • • • •

Irish coffee pudding
Toffee pudding

Upside-down pear pudding

Spring Starters

Artichoke terrine with cream and chive sauce

Let us turn to spring food. Here is a dainty dish to set before a returning hero – from the Auberge de Provence's restaurant book at the St James's Court Hotel in Buckingham Gate. You need a lot of artichokes, a good thing to bring back from a day trip to France.

SERVES 8

4kg (9 lb) globe artichokes
1 teaspoon plain flour
chives
8 egg yolks

1 litre (1¼ pints) crème fraîche
salt
freshly ground white pepper
whipped cream, to serve

This terrine has to sit for 12 hours, so make it the day before you want it. Preheat the oven to 200°C/400°F/Gas 6.

Prepare a *bain-marie*: select a rectangular oven-proof dish or roasting tin big enough to contain the terrine. Fill it with water to a depth of 3cm (1¼ inches) and place a sheet of newspaper folded in two on the bottom of the dish or tin to prevent the water from boiling during the cooking. Place the dish in the oven and raise the heat to its highest setting until you put the terrine in, when you turn it down again to 200°C etc.

Prepare the artichokes by cutting away the leaves with scissors

15

until only the hearts (*fonds*) are left. Scrape away the hairy chokes with a sharp little knife. Mix the flour with some water and add to a saucepan of boiling salted water, then cook the artichokes in it for about 30 minutes until tender.

Drain the hearts and cut them into slices about 5mm (¼ inch) thick. Arrange these in layers in the bottom of the terrine, adding a few chopped chives between the layers. Beat the egg yolks into the crème fraîche, season to taste and pour over the artichokes. Put the terrine into the oven in the *bain-marie*, turn the heat back to 200°C and cook for 30 minutes. Leave to cool for 12 hours, then unmould and cut into slices.

Serve with whipped cream, adding a few chopped chives before whipping.

Crab au gratin

As a cure for my foot warts, I am having to bind each toe in fresh banana skins every day, so I have been trying to find ways of using the fruit as I don't particularly like a plain banana, or even one with cream as did that naughty father of Auberon Waugh. One method I have found palatable is to cover them in a lime and oil vinaigrette with the addition of a lot of Worcestershire sauce, rather as though they were avocados. This also went very well with a fish curry. The following receipt is another good way of using them up.

SERVES 4

1 good tablespoon butter	grated nutmeg (optional)
1 good tablespoon plain flour	50ml (2 fluid oz) medium sherry
300ml (½ pint) single cream	450g (1 lb) crab meat (brown and white)
75g (3 oz) freshly grated Parmesan cheese	anchovy essence
salt	4 tablespoons fresh breadcrumbs
freshly ground black pepper	extra butter
Tabasco	4 bananas

Make a béchamel sauce by combining the butter and flour in a pan and cooking gently for a couple of minutes; then stir in the cream, a little at a time, and increase the heat until the sauce thickens. When ready stir in most of the cheese, reserving some for sprinkling later. When it is mixed and melted, season well with the salt and pepper and a good dash or so of Tabasco and maybe a little grated nutmeg. Add the sherry, then stir in the crab meat, adding a little anchovy essence to suit your taste. Put the mixture into a shallow gratin dish.

Mix the breadcrumbs with the remaining cheese and sprinkle all over the top. Dot with butter and grill until nice and brown.

Peel the bananas, cut them in half lengthways and fry in 40g (1½ oz) of butter. Serve with the crab.

The Milford salad

If you prefer to eat your pears in a natural state, try this.

SERVES 4

4 ripe pears, peeled and quartered
1 bunch of watercress

For the dressing:

75g (3 oz) roquefort cheese
4 tablespoons olive oil

1½ tablespoons cider vinegar
freshly ground black pepper

Mash the roquefort cheese in a bowl with a fork. Add the other ingredients and mix well — a quick whizz in a food processor seems to work. Adjust the seasoning, remembering that roquefort is very salty.

Lay the pears on a bed of watercress, cover with the dressing and serve. Lord Carnarvon was taught to make this by his French governess, Mlle Marcelle Huc, or 'Doll' to the family, so *bon appétit* to you all.

Maccheroncini with mussels

Much as I love *Spaghetti con Vongole* (clams, cockles), I detest
the grit that seems inseparable from those bought here, except for the
very expensive tinned Italian ones. A great dish of pasta and mussels,
however, is gritless and equally delicious. Mussels are fine and
plentiful, so use them.

SERVES 8

750g (1 ½ lb) maccheroncini
2 large fresh tomatoes
1.75kg (4 lb) mussels in their shells
1 tablespoon olive oil

1 onion, chopped finely
75g (3 oz) butter
1 level tablespoon plain flour
salt and freshly ground pepper

Dip the tomatoes into boiling water for half a minute, peel, remove
seeds and liquid. Chop the flesh finely.

Clean and scrub the mussels, removing any beards and seaweed
and discarding any that are broken or open. Put the oil in a large pan,
then the mussels, cover with a lid and fry briskly until all the mussels
are open. Take the mussels from their shells and keep on one side. Pass
the liquid from the pan through a sieve lined with butter muslin and
reserve. There should be a good 300ml (½ pint): if not, top up with
boiling water.

Gently fry the onion in the butter for two minutes, add the flour,
and fry for another half minute. Add the mussel liquid little by little,
stirring all the time until smooth: bring the whole lot to the boil, add
the tomatoes, and season with salt and freshly ground pepper. Bring to
the boil again and then simmer gently for a further 12 minutes.

Meanwhile cook the maccheroncini in a large pan of boiling salted water. Now add the mussels to the tomato sauce for a moment,
merely to heat through, then pour over the cooked maccheroncini,
which you have drained into a warm serving dish. Mix well with two
forks and serve.

La Ribollita

On 25 March, we celebrate the greatest event in history, the Incarnation of
Our Lord on the feast of the Annunciation of the Blessed Virgin Mary, when the
Archangel Gabriel addressed her with the words: 'Hail, full of grace, the Lord is with
thee,' and so He was and thus commenced Christianity. To prepare for glorious Easter,
I always think a hefty, meatless soup is suitable for abstaining adults. I was reminded
of this famous Tuscan soup at the River Café the other day, where a bunch of us were
assembled for an olive oil tasting. The soup should really be made with the Italian
black cabbage, but unless you grow it yourself it is not on the average
vegetable barrow. I use Swiss chard and savoy cabbage instead.

SERVES 8

For the bean cooking:

225g (8 oz) dried cannellini beans
1 tablespoon olive oil – extra virgin
1 celery stalk
2 cloves garlic, peeled
1 medium carrot, scraped

50g (2 oz) salt bacon, prosciutto or
pancetta in one piece (optional, not for
Good Friday)
2.75 litres (5 pints) cold water
rock salt

For the soup:

2 celery stalks
1 large red onion
2 medium carrots, scraped
4 cloves garlic, finely chopped
15 sprigs flat parsley – leaves only
6 tablespoons olive oil
3 large ripe tomatoes, peeled and chopped
piece of dried red chilli
salt and freshly ground pepper

sprig of thyme or ½ teaspoon dried thyme
450g (1 lb) savoy cabbage, cut into 1cm
(½ inch) strips
450g (1 lb) Swiss chard, cut into 2.5cm
(1 inch) strips
2 potatoes, roughly diced
3 cups good stock
8 large slices good crusty bread – stale
extra virgin olive oil, best quality

Soak the beans overnight. Drain and rinse well under running water.
Put the oil into a large saucepan. Add the chopped celery, garlic and
carrot and fry gently for 10 minutes. Mix in the beans and the piece of

19

bacon, then cover with the cold water. Bring to the boil, then simmer very gently until the beans are cooked but not broken (about an hour, depending on the age of the bean). Season with salt, mix well and cook for a further minute. Drain the beans but save the liquid. Put the beans in a bowl and cover with a wet cloth.

For the soup, coarsely chop the celery, onion, carrots, garlic and parsley. Heat the olive oil in the pan, add the choppings and sauté for 10 minutes, stirring with a wooden spoon. Then mix in the tomatoes and chilli and cook for a further five minutes. Pour in the liquid from the beans, season with salt, pepper and thyme, bring to the boil and simmer for 15 minutes. Meanwhile, soak the cabbage, chard and potatoes in cold water, drain and add to the soup. Cook for 45 minutes, adding stock if needed, though the soup should be rather thick. Add the beans for the last five minutes.

In a large earthenware or Pyrex bowl arrange a layer of the bread, then ladle soup on top of it; repeat this until all the bread and the soup are used up. Let it cool, then cover and refrigerate. The next day reheat the ribollita and serve in big soup plates at room temperature, with fresh olive oil poured over each serving. This is a wonderful soup and the perfect vehicle for really good olive oil.

Asparagus and smoked salmon tarts

The asparagus is with us for its only too short stay – the real British sort, which I still think has the best flavour, is in season from May for 4–6 weeks only, and really needs nothing but good melted butter or Hollandaise, but if you have a few stalks over, these little tarts from *The Hungry Monk* are exciting little first courses or supper dishes.

SERVES 4

225g (8 oz) rich shortcrust pastry
6 good size spears of asparagus
175g (6 oz) smoked salmon
a few sprigs of fresh dill
1 whole egg

1 egg yolk
150ml (¼ pint) milk
150ml (¼ pint) double cream
salt and freshly ground black pepper

Preheat the oven to 200°C/400°F/Gas 6.

You need six little tart tins with loose bottoms, 10cm (4 inches) in diameter and 3cm (1¼ inches) deep. Roll out the pastry on a floured board and line the tins with it. Line the pastry with greaseproof paper and a layer of dried beans or rice, place on a baking tray and bake in the preheated oven for 10–15 minutes or until the visible edges of the pastry are just turning gold. Remove the paper and the beans or rice and cook again until the base is just crisp. Remove from the oven, cool and remove from the tins carefully in readiness for their fillings. Reduce the heat of the oven to 190°C/375°F/Gas 5.

Trim off 2.5cm (1 inch) from the base of the asparagus spears. Steam or poach for about 5–8 minutes until tender, keeping the heads out of the water. Drain. Cut 7.5cm (3 inches) off the tips and reserve for decoration. Roughly chop the remainder.

Finely chop the smoked salmon and the dill. Put the eggs in a bowl with the milk and cream, whisk well. Tip in the smoked salmon and dill, season with salt and pepper.

Place the chopped asparagus in equal parts on the base of the pastry cases and then equally fairly pour in the salmon and egg mixture. Put an asparagus tip on each. Place on a baking tray and cook for 20 to 30 minutes until set and golden on top.

These are delicious served with watercress or, if you are feeling energetic, make a sweet pepper sauce by cooking three de-seeded, finely chopped pimentos in a covered saucepan with a splash of white wine vinegar, a glass of dry sherry and a little water. Cook until soft, season with salt and pepper, sieve or whizz and serve warm.

Chilled tomato soup with frozen extra virgin olive oil

Antony Worrall Thompson, another of our British chefs, has produced a cookbook: *Modern Bistro Cookery*. It is a splendid book of robust, seasonal Mediterranean-style receipts. Here is one – a terrific spring starter.

SERVES 4

For the olive oil cubes:

extra virgin olive oil

For the pesto:

100g (4 oz) basil leaves
2 large cloves of garlic, peeled
100 g (4 oz) freshly grated Parmesan
cheese

25g (1 oz) pine nuts
extra virgin olive oil

For the soup:

2 slices white country bread

1 tablespoon sherry vinegar

1 clove of garlic, peeled and finely chopped

2 teaspoons caster sugar

1 red chilli, de-seeded and finely chopped

50ml (2 fluid oz) extra virgin olive oil

450g (1 lb) plum tomatoes, peeled and de-seeded

1 tablespoon best-quality tomato ketchup

450ml (15 fluid oz) good tomato juice

4 spring onions, finely sliced

1 sweet red pepper, roasted, peeled, de-seeded and diced

½ large cucumber, peeled, de-seeded and roughly diced

salt and freshly ground pepper

8 basil leaves, torn

To make the olive oil cubes, half-fill eight sections of an ice tray with extra virgin olive oil.

For the pesto, put the basil leaves, garlic cloves, Parmesan cheese and pine nuts in a blender, with enough olive oil to make a purée. Blend until smooth. This will make about 275g (10 oz) of pesto, so you will have plenty left over, which will keep happily in a jar in the refrigerator.

To make the soup, cut the crusts off the bread, tear it into pieces and place in a food processor or blender. With the machine running, add the vinegar, garlic, sugar and chilli, and blend until smooth. Add the liquid olive oil until the bread will absorb no more; then, a little at a time, add the tomatoes, ketchup, tomato juice, spring onions, red pepper, cucumber and 1 tablespoon of pesto. Continue to blend to form a smooth emulsion. Season to taste with salt and pepper. Chill.

Pour into brightly coloured terracotta bowls and, just before serving, garnish with the frozen olive oil cubes and the torn basil leaves.

Spring Main Courses

Coq au Riesling

**As a sop to Cerberus, here is a nice little chicken dish
cooked with wine, the lighter alternative to *Coq au Vin* where red
wine is usually used. This is made with white.**

·· S E R V E S 6 ··

6 skinned chicken breasts
1 tablespoon sunflower oil
40g (1½ oz) butter
20 baby onions

20 button mushrooms
½ bottle Alsace Riesling, warmed
150ml (¼ pint) thick cream
salt and freshly ground pepper

Fry the breasts gently in the oil and butter until just browning.
Remove from the pan with a slotted spoon and keep warm, then fry
the onions and mushrooms. Return the breasts to the pan and pour the
warmed wine over all. Simmer for 15 minutes until tender.

Remove everything except the wine juices from the pan and
keep warm. Bring the wine and juices to the bubble; add the cream,
boil rapidly to reduce the sauce; season well with salt and freshly
ground pepper; pour over the chicken, onions and mushrooms and
serve piping hot with some steamed, shredded white cabbage and
little boiled potatoes.

Lamb stew with flageolet beans

I have been pondering the fate of poor St Agatha, patroness of Sicily whose breasts were torn off during her martyrdom as she had already overcome the evil solicitations and insistence of the governor of Catania. What a tale. I think we should remember her in some way – breast of lamb perhaps, but it is too fatty, so let us have a comforting stew. I have been playing around with my succulent lamb shanks again. Frankly I think lamb (oh that it were mutton) stews better than beef, which is apt to go stringy.

.... SERVES 8 ....

400g (14 oz) dried flageolet beans

1.5kg (3½ lb) boned shoulder of lamb

3.4 litres (6 pints) cold water

2 onions

2 cloves

1 leek

3 little bouquets garnis, each made up of a sprig of thyme, 4 sprigs of parsley, a small piece of celery and a bayleaf tied with a thread

salt and pepper

4 lambs' shanks or trotters (sheep's feet)

juice of 2 lemons

3.4 litres (6 pints) boiling water

3.4 litres (6 pints) cold water

1 tablespoon plain flour mixed to a thin cream with water

3 litres (5½ pints) cold water

4 carrots

1 tablespoon peppercorns

300ml (½ pint) double cream

3 tablespoons Dijon mustard

4 egg yolks

chopped parsley and chervil

Soak the beans 12 hours in advance of cooking. Remove as much fat as possible from the lamb and cut into largish chunks. Put the chunks into a bowl of iced water and chill in the refrigerator for 12 hours, changing the water once or twice. This draws the blood from the meat and whitens it.

Drain the soaked beans and cook in 3.4 litres (6 pints) of cold water with one of the onions stuck with the cloves, the leek and one

25

of the bouquets garnis. Bring to the boil, then simmer gently for about 2 hours. Skim frequently, adding salt after the first hour.

Rub the shanks or trotters with lemon juice and plunge into the boiling water for 10 minutes, then remove them and run under a cold tap. Remove hooves if you are using trotters. Cook in the 3.4 litres (6 pints) of cold water to which you have added the juice of 1 lemon, the flour and water mix, 2 carrots, another bouquet and a few of the peppercorns. Cook for about 2 hours but don't over-cook.

While all this is cooking, drain the chunks of lamb and again put them to cook in a saucepan of 1 litre (5½ pints) of cold water to which you can add a good beef stock cube, if you like, 2 peeled carrots, 1 onion, a few peppercorns and the final bouquet. Add a little salt and cook gently for 1½ hours.

When the shanks or trotters are cooked, drain them and allow to cool. Remove skin and bones and cut into fairly large pieces. When the lamb is cooked remove the pieces from the pan then turn up the heat until you have reduced the liquid to a mere 1 litre (1¾ pints). Put the lamb and the shanks into a flame-proof earthenware casserole and keep hot while you make the sauce.

Mix the cream, Dijon mustard and egg yolks in a bowl, add the reduced liquid from the lamb, whisking thoroughly, then pour the mixture into a saucepan. Heat very gently; use a heat deflector if you have one, but for heaven's sake don't scramble the sauce. Whisk all the time, adjust the seasoning and, just before it reaches the boil, remove from the heat and strain through a fine wire sieve over the pieces of lamb in the casserole.

Drain the beans and remove the various bits of vegetables and bouquet, which have been cooking with them. Stir the beans into the 'blanquette'. Heat them briefly to make sure everything is piping hot, sprinkle with chopped parsley and chervil. Serve with a red Bordeaux I should think, and a salad afterwards.

You can replace the flageolet beans in this dish with other kinds of dried beans or even fresh or frozen broad beans which will take no time at all.

This may sound rather complicated but once you have everything on the go, it is all very simple.

Ragout of lamb

For spring, I thought we would have England's answer to *navarin printanier*. This is a delicious dish, originally from dear Michael Smith.

SERVES 4

1kg (2 lb) boned leg of lamb
2 heaped tablespoons seasoned flour
olive oil
½ teaspoon cayenne pepper
2 large cloves of garlic, crushed
sprig of rosemary
grated rind of a lemon
2 carrots, diced
½ large head of celery, diced

1 litre (1¼ pints) chicken stock
18 pickling onions or large
spring onions
30g (1¼ oz) butter
1½ teaspoons caster sugar
5 large, firm, tasty tomatoes
salt and freshly ground pepper
1 heaped tablespoon chopped parsley
or basil

Cut the meat into 3.5cm (1½ inch) cubes. Shake them in a plastic bag with half the seasoned flour until coated. Heat the olive oil in a pan, brown the meat briskly, and transfer to a casserole. Sprinkle the meat with the rest of the flour and any left in the bag. Add the cayenne, garlic, rosemary and grated lemon rind. In the pan you cooked the meat in, brown the carrots and the celery lightly, then add to the casserole with the lamb, etc. Pour on the stock, bring to simmering point, cover and cook for 1½ hours or until tender but not overcooked, either on top of the stove or in the oven at 190°C/375°F/Gas 5.

Prepare the onions, leaving 2.5cm (1 inch) of green if using the spring onions or removing the skin from the pickling ones (this is facilitated by pouring some boiling water over them and leaving for 30 seconds or so). Melt half the butter in a small frying-pan and turn the onions in it, sprinkle with the sugar and cook until they are lightly caramelised. Shake them about to colour evenly. Add to the ragout about 45 minutes before the end of cooking.

Skin the tomatoes, cut them across and scoop out the seeds. Chop roughly. When the ragout is done, skim off any excess fat, check the seasoning and transfer to a fine, warm serving dish. Heat the tomatoes in the remaining butter, then pour over the lamb. Strew the basil or parsley or both over all. Serve with baked potatoes.

Turkey loaf

I have noticed they have now taken to selling turkey mince in supermarkets – I created the following concoction out of curiosity and found it remarkably good, and it certainly produces a very reasonable supper or picnic dish.

SERVES 4

10g (1¼ oz) dried porcini mushrooms –
or 100g (¼ lb) fresh mushrooms
450g (1 lb) turkey mince
225g (8 oz) best-quality sausage meat
225g (8 oz) turkey livers
3 plump cloves of garlic
10 juniper berries

1 medium onion
½ teaspoon each of sage and thyme
a crushed bayleaf
salt and freshly ground pepper
1 egg
150ml (¼ pint) good poultry stock
streaky bacon, about 225g (8 oz)

Preheat the oven to 180°C/350°F/Gas 4.

If you are using the porcini mushrooms, soak them in a little water and milk for 30 minutes.

Place the mince and the sausage meat in a large bowl. Chop finely or process the liver, mushrooms, garlic, juniper berries, onion, herbs and bayleaf. Add to the mince. Season with salt and quite a lot of freshly ground pepper, crack an egg into the mixture and moisten with the stock. Squish everything together until well and thoroughly mixed. Transfer to a terrine or loaf tin 24 x 14 x 7cm (9¼ x 5¼ x 2¾ inches) lined with streaky bacon and bake in the preheated oven for 1 hour 15 minutes.

Serve hot with bread sauce and cranberry jelly if you like, mashed and puréed potatoes and delicious spring greens or leave to get cold and use as a rough pâté.

Trout cooked in leeks

**In celebration of St David's day, or any bright spring day,
try this dish using the leek. It makes a most luxurious fish dish
to grace any table.**

························· SERVES 4 ·················

4 good-sized fresh trout, gutted and cleaned	freshly ground black pepper
2 teaspoons chopped fresh parsley	8 large but tender leek leaves
salt	8 rashers of streaky bacon, de-rinded
	8 lemon wedges and some parsley sprigs

Preheat the oven to 180°C/350°F/Gas 4. It is quite handy to have the backbone removed from the trout for this receipt. It is not a difficult task: ask your fishmonger to oblige. Alternatively open up the fish, skin side facing you, and press your fingers firmly along the backbone; this will encourage it to break away from the flesh. Now turn it over and with a sharp knife cut the backbone through at the head end and the tail end, then tease it away from the flesh, taking care to remove all the bones.

Sprinkle some parsley, salt and pepper into the cavity of each fish. Wash the leek leaves and wrap two round each trout. Do the same with the bacon (no washing). Secure with a tooth-pick if necessary. Place the fish close together in a gratin dish and bake in the preheated oven for 20 minutes when the bacon should be crisp and the trout cooked.

Serve with lemon wedges and a few sprigs of parsley for colour.

Oxtail with prunes

The feast day of poor old demoted Saint George on 23 April seems to
go by with hardly a whimper, maybe a few red roses in button-holes but no
great festivities such as are held in other parts of the British Isles for their
patron saints. I wonder why. Beloved Albion was the ancient name for the
British Isles, so called because the Romans connected it with *albus*, meaning
white, with reference to the chalk cliffs of Dover. Many foreign chefs have made
a boo-boo using the name in describing dishes of a brown colour and it is often
wrongly applied to a brown soup. The correct Albion soups include a white fish
consommé thickened with tapioca and garnished with shreds of lobster or
a rich white poultry potage with pea-sized balls of carrot and
cucumber floating therein.
All through Lent I hanker for rich, brown oxtail, so this Easter Saturday
I rushed out and bought some fine specimens and a bunch of ravishing young
turnips from the market. I concocted the dish with the addition of prunes and
found it richly rewarding. A good hearty dinner for Saint George, I feel.

SERVES 6

2.25–2.75kg (5–6 lb) oxtail
175g (6 oz) salt pork or unsmoked bacon
4 medium onions
4 large carrots
4 celery stalks
a bouquet of 2 bay leaves, parsley, thyme
and 2 crushed garlic cloves

salt, pepper, mace and allspice
400g (14 oz) tin of chopped tomatoes
300ml (½ pint) Guinness or stout
275g (10 oz) prunes (ready to eat)
1 tablespoon each of Worcestershire
sauce, mushroom ketchup and
tomato purée

Buy the pork or bacon in a piece, remove the rind and cut the meat
into small dice. Chop the onions and slice the carrots and celery. Put
the diced pork into the bottom of a large, heavy casserole, cover with
the chopped vegetables and cook on a very low heat for about 10 minutes until the fat from the pork is beginning to melt and run. Arrange
the pieces of oxtail neatly on top, enclose the bouquet garni in a scrap
of butter muslin and plunge it into the middle. Season the meat with

salt, pepper, mace and allspice. Cover the pot and cook gently for about 30 minutes.

Preheat the oven to 140°C/275°F/Gas 1.

Heat the tomatoes and Guinness together in a little saucepan until they come to the boil. Place the prunes on top of the oxtail and pour over the tomato and Guinness mixture. When the contents of the pot are just bubbling, cover with a sheet of foil and the lid, place in the oven and cook for 4 hours until the meat is practically falling off the bones, which is essential with oxtail.

Using a slotted spoon, fish out the tail pieces and put them on a plate, then put all the juice and vegetables through a food mill. Return this sauce to the casserole, add the Worcestershire sauce, the mushroom ketchup and the tomato purée. Mix thoroughly and check the seasoning. Cool, then leave in the refrigerator until the fat has risen to the top and solidified. Remove the fat and restore the pieces of oxtail to the sauce. Heat gently on top of the stove until all is mixed well together, then finish off in a low oven until piping hot.

This can all take place over two days to suit your convenience. I should serve with a good potato purée and little buttered turnips with a good cutting of chives, tarragon and parsley sprinkled over them. Excellent.

This amount would be enough for six hungry people but if you had a scant few pieces left over for another day you could paint them with melted butter, coat them with breadcrumbs, heat in the oven, then grill until brown and crisp. Serve with a vinaigrette or some of the left-over sauce and a salad.

Steamed chicken

In the run-up to Easter, as part of my Lenten diet, I have taken to steaming chicken, which melts a lot of the fat away. I have a huge steamer left over from an Aga but you can set up a steamer in a pan or a wok with a rack in it.

SERVES 6

1 good (free range) chicken, about 1.5kg (3 lb)

juice of 1 lemon, retaining the pulp

1 tablespoon sea salt

fresh tarragon or any herb you fancy

spring onions

For the sauce:

2 teaspoons soy sauce

pinch of sugar

½ teaspoon salt

2 tablespoons fresh ginger, finely chopped

5 tablespoons spring onions, finely chopped

2 tablespoons peanut oil

1 teaspoon sesame oil

Place the chicken on a heat-proof plate which will fit the steamer. Rub all over and inside with lemon juice, then with the sea salt. Set aside for 15 minutes. Put some fresh herbs and sliced spring onions into the cavity together with the remains of the lemon. Bring the water in the steamer to simmering point. Put the chicken, breast down, into the top half of the steamer or on its plate over the rack. Cover the steamer tightly and gently steam over a medium heat for an hour.

When ready, place on a carving board and, if seriously fasting, remove all skin and any remaining fat and eat with steamed, suitable vegetables: broccoli, courgette, cabbage etc.

Alternatively, you can make a dipping sauce. Mix the soy sauce, sugar, salt, ginger and spring onions in a bowl. In a small pan heat the peanut oil and the sesame oil until they smoke. Pour over the contents of the bowl and serve with the chicken.

Fillet à la Meerlust with potato salad

Now for solid meat. I have a kind fan in Johannesburg, who sent me the *Cape* cookery book. I don't know the names of half the things in it, but this is an entirely new (to me) method of serving beef fillet. The receipt is for a whole fillet, but that would cost about £50 here so I have whittled it down to suit my purse. Meat is very cheap in South Africa.

SERVES 4

450g (1 lb) piece fillet steak
1 clove garlic, crushed
juice of 1 large lemon

1 teaspoon dry mustard
freshly ground salt and pepper
175ml (6 fluid oz) olive oil

Brown the piece of fillet in a hot, cast-iron frying pan just wiped with a bit of oil. The inside should remain raw. Allow to cool. Cut into thin slices and arrange on a suitable dish.

In a jar combine the crushed garlic, lemon juice, mustard, salt, pepper and olive oil. Shake vigorously and pour over the meat. There must be enough sauce to moisten all the meat. Marinate for at least 6 hours, turning occasionally. It goes a terrible colour but is splendid to eat.

Serve with a potato salad dressed with olive oil, lemon juice, garlic and strewn with parsley, chives and grated lemon peel garnished with watercress.

Sea bass with black olives

**A robust fish dish which should be made with sea bass (but many
other types of fish such as sole, monk or John Dory could be used or good
old coley, which is far cheaper and excellent, though despised by foolish folk),
this is an Italian receipt full of flavour and goodness.**

SERVES 4

150g (5 oz) black olives, stoned
2 sprigs fresh thyme
100g (4 oz) fine semolina for coating
450g (1 lb) fillet of fish, boned and
skinned

200g (7 oz) peeled potatoes
3 shallots
3 tablespoons extra virgin olive oil
salt and freshly ground pepper
a few basil leaves

Pound the olives until you have a rough sort of paste. Pull the leaves
off the thyme and mix with the semolina. Cut the fish into four equal
portions. Cover one side with the olive paste, then coat the whole
thing with the semolina. Reserve in the refrigerator.

Cook the potatoes in boiling, salted water, drain them and pass
through a mouli or sieve. Chop the shallots finely and melt them in
some olive oil in a saucepan. When soft, but not browned, add the
potato, salt and pepper and more oil to taste. Keep warm.

Fry the fish in a little oil for about 3 minutes on each side.
Arrange the fish on top of the potatoes. Serve hot with a few fried basil
leaves.

Fish with spring vegetables

**I once had a most delicious dish of fish cooked by my friend
Julian Barran, very suitable for this time of year.**

SERVES 6

900g (2 lb) firm white fish
(sole, monk, John Dory, turbot
or bass etc)
1 medium carrot
1 leek – white part only
the inside of a head of celery

1 medium potato
20 tiny French beans
1 bunch chives
salt and pepper
25g (1 oz) butter
120ml (4 fluid oz) double cream

Try to get a good fishmonger to fillet and skin whichever fish you use, especially if it is the splendid John Dory, which is quite tricky.

Cut the fillets into finger-size strips. Peel the carrot and trim the leek and celery heart. Wash thoroughly and cut into julienne strips the size of matchsticks. Peel and wash the potato, then cut into large dice and cook in lightly salted water until tender.

Top and tail the French beans, wash and cook in a large pan of boiling, salted water for about 5 minutes. Remove from the heat, drain and refresh in cold water. Drain again and reserve on one side on a cloth. Chop the chives finely.

Now to cook. Put the julienne vegetables into a small saucepan with a pinch of salt, 3 tablespoons of water and a teaspoon of butter. Cover and cook briskly until the carrots are tender and the water has almost evaporated. These strips should still have a bite to them and the whole operation should take about 8 minutes. Keep warm.

Pour the cream into a saucepan, add a little salt and the strips of fish. Bring to the boil, turn down the heat and simmer for 2 minutes. Strain the cream into a liquidiser and place the fillets in the pan with the julienne strips and the beans, which should be quite dry; keep warm. Add half the diced potatoes to the cream in the liquidiser and whizz until you have a smooth, light sauce; add more potato if it seems too thin. Add the remaining butter, season to taste and blend again.

Pour the sauce over the fish and vegetables in the saucepan, bring to the boil rapidly, stir in the chopped chives and serve immediately. I know it sounds complicated, but once you have everything at the ready it is quite easy and the velvety, natural sauce is a treat.

Feijoda

In early March there are some saints with splendid names, starting with St Cunegund, married to Duke Henry of Bavaria who became Holy Roman Emperor in 1014. He died in 1024, whereupon the Empress Cunegund took off her imperial regalia and replaced them with the habit of a nun. She founded a nunnery for Benedictines at Kassel, having vowed to do so some time before, when she recovered from a near-fatal illness. St Chrodegang saved Pope Stephen II from exile and brought him over the Alps where Pepin the Short welcomed him to France; and St Fridolin was an Irish wanderer who found the body of Hilary of Poitiers and started a school for young boys on an island in the Rhine and happily encouraged them to play many sports. Such excitement they all got up to.

Excitement of a different sort, this is a wonderful kind of Brazilian cassoulet which takes time but is well worth the effort.

SERVES 8–10

400g (14 oz) *carne seca* (dried beef) or bresaola
900g (2 lb) black beans
bicarbonate of soda
400g (14 oz) salted neck end of pork
400g (14 oz) salted pork belly
400g (14 oz) smoked neck end of pork
400g (14 oz) smoked pork belly

400g (14 oz) linguiça (smoked sausage), or chorizo or kabanos
3 large onions, finely chopped
3 big cloves of garlic, crushed
1 bouquet garni
salt
freshly ground black pepper
vegetable oil

Having found all these ingredients, start cooking the night before consumption. If you can't find dried beef, use some thick bacon, pigs' trotters or ears, or even good black pudding. Soak the beans in plenty of water with a pinch of bicarbonate. Wash all the salted pork under running water in a separate container. Treat the beef or bacon the same way.

Next day wash the meats again and place them in a large casserole together with the smoked meats, minus the sausage. Cover with cold water and bring slowly to the boil. Remove scum and gently simmer for two hours. Add the sausage 45 minutes before the end.

Meanwhile, rinse and boil the black beans for 10 minutes. Drain and return to the rinsed-out saucepan with two of the onions, two of the cloves of garlic and the bouquet garni. Season with the pepper only. Cover with plenty of fresh water, bring to the boil and simmer for 1½ hours.

Once cooked, cut the meats into medium-sized pieces and slice the sausage into large chunks. Take a ladle of the black beans and reserve. Place the rest of the drained beans with the meats in a large casserole and simmer for 45 minutes.

Fifteen minutes before the end, fry the remaining onion and garlic in oil, and season with salt and pepper. Drain the reserved ladle of beans and add them to the pan, crushing them with a fork or a wooden spoon. Add a small cup of the cooking juices from the casserole, stir and reduce, then add to the meats and beans. If it becomes too dry, add a little hot water.

This dish should be accompanied by dry fluffy rice like basmati or patna, usually fried with chopped onion and garlic before adding the water (double the amount of water to rice).

Spring Accompaniments

Creamy mushroom and potato gratin

Now for a really good Lenten dish to be eaten on its own or as a perfect partner to any plain meat or fish. It is from a dear little book about mushrooms by Michael McLaughlin. These are rather grand mushrooms but you can use others, including the wonderful dried porcini, for flavour.

········· SERVES 8 ·········

100g (4 oz) unsalted butter

450g (1 lb) fresh shiitake mushrooms, sliced

450g (1 lb) fresh oyster mushrooms, sliced

2 teaspoons salt

1.5kg (3 lb) baking potatoes, peeled and thinly sliced

freshly ground black pepper

350ml (12 fluid oz) homemade chicken stock

250ml (8 fluid oz) crème fraîche or double cream

See that an oven rack is in the middle of the oven and preheat to 190°C/375°F/Gas 5.

Butter a shallow (6cm [2½ inch] sides) gratin dish or casserole large enough to take all the ingredients. Use 25g (1 oz) of the butter.

In a large frying pan over a medium heat melt 50g (2 oz) of the butter until it foams, add the mushrooms and a teaspoon of salt and

38

cook, tossing and turning until the mushrooms begin to ooze their juices, about five minutes. Remove from the heat and cool to room temperature.

In a large bowl, toss together the mushrooms, their juices and the potatoes (the best way to slice them is on a mandolin if you have one), the remaining teaspoon of salt and a good grinding of black pepper. Transfer to the prepared gratin dish and spread evenly. In another bowl whisk the chicken stock and the crème fraîche or the cream together. Pour this mixture evenly over the contents of the gratin dish, lifting the potatoes and mushrooms so that the liquid seeps in. Cut the rest of the butter into tiny dice and scatter over the top. Bake, tilting the dish occasionally to distribute the juices evenly, until the potatoes are tender and the top is a splendid brown crust, about one and a half hours.

Remove from the oven and let it rest on a rack for five minutes before serving. This is enough for eight people. Stunning.

Scottish nettle pudding

Nettles should be harvested on a fine day, in the morning after the sun has dried off the dew. The young tops should be plucked before they flower using gloves and scissors. They can be used fresh or dried. Wash the nettle tops well and boil in a little water for about 20 minutes, then chop finely and use with other vegetables in soups, stews and pasta dishes. If you just want soup, proceed as for a spinach or sorrel soup, thickening with flour or potato and adding a good amount of thick cream before serving. Alternatively you could try this curious offering.

SERVES 4

A carrier-bagful of young nettle tops, well washed
1 leek, trimmed and sliced

1 head of broccoli, chopped
75g (3 oz) white rice
salt and freshly ground black pepper

Mix all the ingredients together, season with a little salt and freshly ground black pepper, and place in a muslin bag or thin tea towel. Tie well. Boil in well-salted water for about 20 minutes until the vegetables are cooked. Remove from the cloth and serve with a savoury sauce or gravy as a side dish to accompany anything you fancy.

Banana raita

This delectable salad goes well with any hot, spicy dish.

SERVES 4

3 tablespoons sultanas or seedless raisins
25g (1 oz) blanched slivered almonds
200g (7 oz) natural Greek yoghurt
100ml (3½ fluid oz) each of sour and whipping cream

1 heaped tablespoon honey
1 medium-sized banana, ripe but firm
pinch of salt
6 cardamom pods

Pour boiling water over the sultanas or raisins and two-thirds of the almonds. Leave for 10 minutes. Toast the remaining almonds. Mix the yoghurt and creams with the honey. Stir in the drained raisins and almonds. Slice the banana thinly and add to the mixture with the salt. Take the cardamom seeds from their pods and crush them. Add to the raita a little at a time to suit your taste.

Turn into some charming dish, scatter with the toasted almonds and chill for an hour. It is important not to add the banana more than an hour before the meal, or it will lose its bite and the raita will become soggy.

Vegetables with herb cream

Another good spring idea is Elisabeth Luard's accompaniment.

SERVES 4

150ml (¼ pint) whipping cream, lightly whipped
1 tablespoon mild mustard
6 spring onions, chopped
generous handful of fresh herbs, including parsley

salt
900g (2 lb) mixed young vegetables (new potatoes, baby beetroot with leaves attached, baby carrots and leeks, young green beans etc)

Mix the lightly whipped cream with the mustard, spring onions and chopped herbs. Salt to taste. Trim and rinse the vegetables, leave whole. Cook the new potatoes and drain. Cook the other vegetables in boiling salted water for a few minutes until *al dente*. Arrange all the well-drained items on a warm dish and cover or serve with the cream sauce.

41

Potatoes and black olives

There is a very nice *Vegetable Market Cook Book* by Robert Budwig
(lovely name) where I found a dish of simple potatoes and black olives,
perfect for Good Friday and excellent with fish.
If you live in the wilds and cannot buy the prepared olives, marinate
them yourself, but they must be done at least 24 hours in advance. Pack ordinary
black olives into a glass jar with a tightly fitting lid. Add a tablespoon of good olive
oil and a tablespoon of mixed herbes de Provence. Leave for 24 hours, giving the
jar a good shake every hour or so. When the olives are used up you can use
the oil and juices as the base of an interesting salad dressing.

SERVES 6

200g (7 oz) black olives with herbs
2 tablespoons virgin olive oil
8 cloves garlic, peeled and roughly
chopped

4 bay leaves
900g (2 lb) small waxy potatoes, peeled
and diced
sea salt and freshly ground black pepper

Get the best-quality black olives preserved with herbs at some good
delicatessen.

Heat the olive oil in a terracotta or cast-iron pot over a moderate heat and add the garlic, olives and bay leaves. Stir and cook for 5
minutes. Mix in the potatoes, season to taste and pour in about an inch
of water. Cook covered for 20 minutes until the potatoes are tender.
Serve immediately.

Banana and bacon rolls

St Zita is the patron saint of the kitchen and domestics, a must for all households which aspire to good food. She was a dear little saint, a servant herself in a rich household in the Tuscan city of Lucca, where she tended to give the food provided for her to the beggars and impoverished of the town. Her master found this deeply irritating, particularly once, during a famine, when she gave away much of the family supply of beans, though when he inspected the bean cupboard they had miraculously been replaced; wasn't that nice? And this is a nice little dish which even children will eat.

SERVES I

1 banana per person
1 good long rasher streaky bacon (rindless)

1 slice bread or baguette to fit the banana
butter to fry the bread

Peel the banana and cut it in half. Stretch the rasher of bacon with the back of a knife and cut in half. Wind the bacon round the halves of bananas and secure with a cocktail stick if necessary. Grill the banana for 7–10 minutes, turning from time to time until the bacon is crisp and the banana is soft within. Meanwhile fry the bread crisply in the butter, pile the banana rolls on top, remove any cocktail sticks and serve. Good with a tomato salad.

Spring Desserts

Irish coffee pudding

With St Patrick's day in mind, here is a Gaelic treat, handed down through an Irish family. Although I don't see any reason not to have it on other days as well.

SERVES 4

4 eggs
100g (4 oz) caster sugar, or less if preferred
300ml (½ pint) very strong cold coffee (espresso)

3 tablespoons Irish whiskey
scant 15g (½ oz) gelatine
300ml (½ pint) double or whipping cream
extra whipped cream and chopped walnuts

Separate the eggs. Put the yolks and half the sugar into a bowl. Whisk until quite smooth, then add three-quarters of the coffee. Stand the bowl over a saucepan of hot but not boiling water and stir briskly until you achieve a thickened custard which will coat the back of the spoon. Mix in the whiskey.

Sprinkle the gelatine into the rest of the coffee and let it stand for 5 minutes, then dissolve it over hot water. Blend with the coffee custard and leave to cool and stiffen slightly.

Whip the cream into peaks. Whisk the egg whites until stiff, then fold in the remaining sugar. Fold the cream and then the egg whites into the jellied mixture and spoon the lot into a lovely dish or six separate ones. Chill and set, top with cream and walnuts. Yum.

Toffee Pudding

Here is a simple, quickly made pudding from Miranda Barran who says it is a great way of silencing children and in-laws if you over-cook the toffee.

······································· SERVES 4 ·······································

4–6 slices good white bread
enough milk to soak the bread
100g (4 oz) butter
50g (2 oz) demerara sugar

2 tablespoons golden syrup
generous squeeze of lemon juice
whipped cream

Remove the crusts, cut the bread into 5cm (2 inch) squares and soak in the milk.

Put the butter, sugar, golden syrup and lemon juice in a heavy-bottomed frying pan. Heat gently until the sugar is quite dissolved, then turn up the heat a bit until the whole mass starts turning into brown liquid toffee.

Put the bread squares into the toffee, then pile neatly (impossible) on to a hot dish. Pour over the remaining toffee and serve very hot with piles of whipped cream.

45

Upside-down pear pudding

I went to a terrific lunch at the Four Seasons Hotel, Park Lane, where the
Earl and Countess of Carnarvon were presiding and Mark Greenfield, the Highclere
Castle chef, was cooking dishes from their second book of receipts. Everything
was delicious so I thought to include a pudding from the book.

SERVES 8–10

For the base:

225g (8 oz) soft brown sugar
100g (4 oz) butter

For the contents:

4 ripe pears, peeled, cored and quartered
225g (8 oz) plain flour plus 1 teaspoon
bicarbonate of soda
½ teaspoon salt
4 teaspoons cinnamon
2 teaspoons ground ginger

½ teaspoon grated nutmeg
pinch ground cloves
2 eggs, beaten
175g (6 oz) black treacle
250ml (8 fluid oz) milk
225g (8 oz) butter, melted

Preheat the oven to 180°C/350°F/Gas 4.

To make the base, place the sugar and butter in a saucepan over
a low heat. Once melted, turn up the heat and allow to bubble for a
couple of minutes. Pour into a 25cm (10 inch) oven-proof dish.
Arrange the pears rounded side down on the bottom of the dish.

Thoroughly mix the rest of the ingredients together and pour
over the pears. Bake for one hour in the lower section of the oven.

Test with a sharp, pointed knife which should come out clean; if
it has raw mix sticking to it, the pudding will need further cooking.
Allow to cool slightly before turning it out carefully onto some
gorgeous serving plate. Eat with lightly whipped double cream or
some very good vanilla ice-cream. The black treacle is the inspired
ingredient, I think.

Summer

starters

Mushroom soufflé
Lobster risotto
Tomato aspic ring

Scallop and spinach dainties
Chilled aubergine soup

main courses

Stuffed gurnard
Spiced chicken
Pasticcio di maccheroni
Courgette soufflé
Boeuf à la mode

Cardamom steamed salmon on
bean salad
Gigot of monkfish
Coley mayonnaise
Turkey tonnato

accompaniments

Couscous salad
Puréed basil potatoes
Melanzane a funghetti
Potatoes Ruspoli

Ricotta and beetroot salad
Spinach and potato timbales
Bob Schultz's meatballs

desserts

Amaretti and strawberry terrine
Lemon syllabub with red fruits
Almond cream with berries

Almond meringues
White peaches in redcurrant syrup
Soft meringues with egg custard

Summer Starters

Mushroom soufflé

At the beginning of summer my thoughts turn to a little saint, Petronilla,
who was put to death when she refused to marry a nobleman named Flaccus – I don't
blame her. Petronilla preferred to devote her life to her Saviour and was martyred
for her faith. Legend has it that she was the daughter of St Peter. In the cemetery
of Domitilla, Rome, there is a fresco dating from the fourth century which
shows the poor lass about to be killed.
On a more mundane level, when my refrigerator once broke down,
and I had to wait days before the mechanic could come, I devised a way of
saving some fine great mushrooms that were on the turn. I made them into a
soufflé. I'd never seen a mushroom soufflé, let alone eaten one, but it
was rather good if a slightly sinister colour. Try it.

SERVES 4

4 of those huge field mushrooms
1 medium-sized onion
1 clove garlic
50g (2 oz) butter
salt, freshly ground pepper and nutmeg
2 tablespoons plain flour

150ml (¼ pint) milk, warmed
85ml (3 fluid oz) thick cream
2 whole eggs, separated
2 extra whites of egg
grated gruyère or
Parmesan cheese

Preheat the oven to 220°C/425°F/Gas 7.
Chop the mushrooms, onion and garlic finely. Melt the butter in
a saucepan large enough to take all the ingredients, and stew the

chopped vegetables together with the lid on until they are soft and all the juices are running. Season well with salt, freshly ground pepper and a good scraping of nutmeg.

Stir in the flour and cook gently for a minute, turning the mixture. Add the warmed milk little by little, until you have a thick sauce, stirring all the time, then add the cream. Remove from the heat and add the well-beaten egg yolks, mix together and leave to cool.

Whisk the egg whites (I always have some whites in little pots in the freezer left over from something like mayonnaise) until they stand in peaks. Stir a couple of tablespoons of the whites into the mushroom mixture, then fold in the rest. Turn into a well-buttered 1.75ml (3 pint) soufflé dish and sprinkle with about two tablespoons of the grated cheese.

Put the dish in a baking tin filled with enough water to come half-way up the sides of the dish and place in the centre of the preheated oven for 30 minutes. Don't peek, but serve immediately. Hope you enjoy.

Lobster risotto

Canadian lobsters are flown into the country live from Canada daily. They are really very good, moist and succulent, and not too pricey. Here is a dish that'll make your lobster go a long way.

SERVES 4

50g (2 oz) black-eyed beans
1 x 450g (1 lb) lobster
olive oil
150g (5 oz) butter
25g (1 oz) chopped shallots
1½ tablespoons brandy
100g (4 oz) arborio rice
200ml (⅓ pint) white wine

salt and pepper
2 tablespoons fish stock
200ml (⅓ pint) spicy tomato sauce (*see opposite*)
25g (1 oz) chorizo sausage
25g (1 oz) grated Parmesan cheese
chopped parsley

For the spicy tomato sauce:

1 onion, chopped

1 clove of garlic, chopped

50g (2 oz) chorizo sausage, chopped

2 tablespoons olive oil

50g (2 oz) butter

1 tablespoon tomato purée

handful basil leaves, torn

900g (2 lb) fresh tomatoes, chopped

salt

freshly ground pepper

Wash the beans, soak them overnight, then wash them again before simmering them for two hours until soft.

Blanch the lobster in boiling water for 1½ minutes. Remove from the water, crack the meat from the shell and keep warm.

In a pan, place a tablespoon of olive oil and half the butter and the lobster shells. Fry gently for 5 minutes, add the shallots and sweat until cooked. Flame with the brandy and, when the flame has died down, remove the shells, then add the rice. Stir this until it goes opaque, then add the white wine and a little seasoning. Reduce the wine by half and add half the fish stock and all the tomato sauce (see below). Stir continuously while the rice is cooking, slowly adding the remaining fish stock.

When the rice is cooked, approximately 30 minutes, add the black-eyed beans, chorizo sausage, the rest of the butter and half the Parmesan cheese. Adjust the seasoning. Add the lobster meat in chunks, heat until just cooked, about three minutes, then serve immediately. Sprinkle with chopped parsley and Parmesan.

For the tomato sauce, sweat the chopped onion, garlic clove and chorizo sausage in a mixture of olive oil and butter. When soft, add the tomato purée and basil leaves; cook for 3 minutes. Add the chopped fresh tomatoes. Cook until soft. Liquidise, sieve and season.

Tomato aspic ring

I had this aspic one summer, at the house of Mary Lowe in Newton Reigny, Cumbria. It is spectacular looking, and gleams like a vast bit of amber.

······································· S E R V E S   6 — 8 ·······································

2 packets of Riebers aspic powder
900ml (1½ pints) hot water
2 shallots
olive oil
2 big cloves of garlic, chopped
1 large tin Italian tomatoes (750g/28 oz)

salt and freshly ground black pepper
sugar
Tabasco
plenty of fresh basil (2 handfuls)
fronds of fennel or dill
chopped chives

Dissolve one packet of aspic in 600ml (1 pint) of hot water and dissolve the other packet in a separate bowl in a generous 300ml (½ pint) of hot water. Line a large ring mould with half the 600ml (1 pint) of aspic and set in the refrigerator.

Meanwhile, in a heavy saucepan, soften the shallots in olive oil, add the chopped garlic and tomatoes and season to taste with salt, freshly ground pepper, a little sugar and a dash or so of Tabasco. Heat gently just to break up the tomatoes, then pour into a processor and whizz very briefly, adding some of the basil, fennel or dill and chopped chives. Add the 300ml (½ pint) of the stiffer aspic and leave to cool down.

Scatter more torn basil leaves or any other fresh herbs you fancy onto the set aspic from the refrigerator, then cover with the remaining 300ml (½ pint) of aspic. Reset and when firm pour in the tomato aspic mixture. Chill well until quite set.

Place the mould in some warm water for a moment, then turn out onto a pretty dish. Serve with a good home-made mayonnaise flavoured with garlic and mustard. The insertion of hard-boiled quails' eggs after you have sprinkled the middle with herbs is a nice little bit of excitement to find in the aspic.

54

Scallop and spinach dainties

July sees the feast of St James the Greater, he of the *Coquille Saint-Jacques* and *Santiago de Compostela*, so we'd better have a dish of scallops to honour him.

SERVES 4

2 large onions
25g (1 oz) clarified butter
225g (8 oz) fresh spinach, washed
freshly ground salt and pepper and grated fresh nutmeg
16 large scallops

2 good-sized tomatoes plus one for garnish
5 tablespoons double cream
1 tablespoon lemon juice
fresh chervil, dill or parsley for garnish

Oil six ramekins in readiness. Slice the onions finely, put them in a saucepan with the butter and cook very slowly for two hours until they are a soft mass.

Towards the end of this time preheat the oven to 200°C/400°F/Gas 6. Add the spinach to the pan and cook until tender (five minutes or so). Remove from the pan and roughly chop the mixture, seasoning well with freshly ground salt, pepper and nutmeg gratings.

Slice the scallops vertically into thin rounds and lay them on the bottoms of the ramekins. Cover each one with the spinach mixture and place all the ramekins on a baking tray. Bake in the oven for 5 minutes.

For the sauce, peel and seed the tomatoes and purée them in a liquidiser. Add the cream and lemon juice to the purée. Season and mix well together.

When the ramekins of scallops are ready, turn them out on to a platter and surround with the sauce. Garnish with fine strips of tomato and a sprinkling of chervil, dill or parsley. Very good indeed – the hot scallops and the cold sauce make a delicious combination.

Chilled aubergine soup

This offering is from Catherine Davidson of Glasgow and is an original and interesting soup made from aubergines, which I have adapted. The flavour is light and refreshing, an excellent summer soup and a change from watercress or vichyssoise.

SERVES 4

2 large shiny aubergines
salt
2 onions, chopped
4 tablespoons olive oil
4 cloves garlic
1.2 litres (2 pints) good chicken stock

mace
cinnamon stick
2 tablespoons lemon juice
300ml (½ pint) double cream or Greek yoghurt
parsley, chives or coriander leaves

Cut the aubergines into chunky dice, sprinkle with salt and leave in a colander or sieve for an hour to drain.

Fry the chopped onions in the olive oil in a large saucepan until just browning. Add the garlic crushed with a wooden spoon, and the drained and squeezed aubergines; mix well, cover and cook gently until soft.

Heat the chicken stock with a pinch of mace and a cinnamon stick, then pour into the aubergines and simmer for about 10 minutes. Remove from the heat, add the lemon juice and season to taste. When cool enough, remove cinnamon stick and put the soup through the blender. When cold stir it into the cream or yoghurt.

Serve sprinkled with chopped herbs.

Summer Main Courses

Stuffed gurnard

We keep being told that the Brits are very unadventurous toward fish, and so they are. Have you tried gurnards? Very good firm white flesh, ravishing pink skins and sweet apologetic faces looking like a Jules Verne submarine. I cooked them in the Normandy manner, and they were cheap and excellent.

SERVES 6

6 gurnards (suitable size for one each)
butter
2 small sweet apples, finely sliced
2 large shallots, finely sliced
bouquet garni

300ml (½ pint) dry cider
2 plum tomatoes, sliced
2 tablespoons thick cream
chopped parsley

For the stuffing:

75g (3 oz) butter
275g (10 oz) mushrooms, chopped finely
1 chopped shallot
2 large tablespoons good sausage meat
4cm (1½ inch) slice de-crusted bread

milk
chopped parsley
chopped thyme
lemon juice
salt and pepper

Preheat the oven to 180°C/350°F/Gas 4.
For the stuffing, melt the butter and fry the mushrooms, shallot

and sausage meat gently. Soak the bread in a little milk, squeeze dry and add to the pan. Season with parsley, thyme, lemon juice, salt and pepper. Divide into six and stuff the gutted fish with the mixture.

Butter a fire-proof dish which will accommodate the fish snugly, head to tail. Tuck the finely sliced sweet apple and shallot in between the gurnards and bury the bouquet garni somewhere. Pour the cider over them and lay the tomato slices on top.

Bake in the oven for about 30 minutes. In the last five minutes, drizzle the cream over the fish and strew with a good handful of chopped parsley.

Spiced chicken

There are never enough ways to serve that useful bird the chicken, so let us have a slightly spiced and peppery version. This is very good served on a bed of the *Couscous Salad* on page 69.

SERVES 6

6 chicken pieces of your choice
1 tablespoon paprika
2 tablespoons tomato purée
1 large clove garlic, crushed
1 level teaspoon Maldon or Alpine salt

1 tablespoon Dijon mustard
75g (3 oz) just-melted butter
1 teaspoon sugar
a good pinch of chilli powder or cayenne pepper

Skin the chicken pieces and stab all over with a fork or a sharp little knife. Lay them in a snug dish in one layer. Mix all the rest of the ingredients together into a paste and spread evenly over the chicken. Cover with film or foil and leave to chill for 12–24 hours, the longer the better. Preheat your grill and cook the chicken for about 20 minutes until the juices run clear where the flesh is pierced.

Pasticcio di maccheroni

Do you remember the magnificent description of a traditional
monumental macaroni pie in *The Leopard* by Giuseppe Tomasi de Lampedusa?
A mouthwatering bit of prose if ever there was one:

'The burnished gold of the crusts, the fragrance of sugar and cinnamon
they exuded were but preludes to the delights released from the interior when
the knife broke the crust: first came a spice-laden haze, then the chicken livers,
hard-boiled eggs, sliced ham, chicken and truffles in masses of piping hot, glistening
macaroni to which the meat juice gave an exquisite hue of suede.'

Wow!
These pies are traditionally from Romagna and they are the only
pasta dishes to use the same short pastry as in sweet tarts, i.e. *Pâté Brisé*.
In the original receipts it is not just the chicken livers that are used but also the
cockscombs and testicles, together with the egg tract containing the unlaid eggs
– all quite difficult to secure round my area. However, Willy Landels and I tried
out a pie from his mother's notes, which, like all old scribbles for the cook,
gave no indication of amounts, and the ingredients for the pastry were quite
wrong. Nevertheless, we produced a savoury effort from pigeon, mortadella,
Italian sausage and mushrooms. I now offer you a detailed receipt.

SERVES 8

40g (1½ oz) dried mushrooms
350g (12 oz) macaroni, broken into 7.5cm
(3 inch) lengths
300ml (½ pint) really good meat stock
made properly
100g (4 oz) calves' sweetbreads
100g (4 oz) chicken livers
100g (4 oz) butter

50g (2 oz) prosciutto crudo, cut
very thin
salt and freshly ground pepper
100g (4 oz) freshly grated Parmesan
cheese
150ml (¼ pint) thick béchamel sauce
(see page 61)
1 egg, beaten

59

For the pastry:

350g (12 oz) plain flour	1 egg
150g (5 oz) butter	15g (½ oz) sugar

Preheat the oven to 220°C/425°F/Gas 7.

Start by making the short pastry. Either by hand or in a food processor, knead all the ingredients lightly to form a smooth dough, wrap in a clean, floured cloth and leave to rest in a cool place while you are getting on with the pie, but don't refrigerate. Put the dried mushrooms into tepid water for 20 minutes, drain and chop roughly.

Cook the macaroni in boiling salted water but take them out while they are still very much *al dente*. When drained, put them in a frying pan with half the stock, and cook over a medium heat until they have absorbed the liquid – about two minutes.

Blanch the sweetbreads for three minutes in boiling water, then plunge into a bowl of cold water. Remove the membrane and any hard tendons. Chop roughly with the chicken livers. Put 25g (1 oz) butter in a small frying pan: when just bubbling, fry the livers and sweetbreads very gently for two minutes. Leave on one side.

In another pan fry the mushrooms in 25g (1 oz) butter until tender, about four minutes. Cut the prosciutto with its fat into small strips and add to the chicken liver mixture. Add the mushrooms and the remaining 50g (2 oz) butter. Mix over a very gentle heat until the butter is melted. Season with salt and freshly ground pepper.

Have a cake tin large enough to take all the ingredients; butter it lavishly. Roll out the pastry; line the tin with it, keeping back enough to make the lid. Put the macaroni and the sauce and some of the grated Parmesan cheese in alternate layers into the pastry case; all the sauce should be used up and the last layer should be covered with the béchamel sauce and the rest of the Parmesan. Place the pastry lid on top and pinch it in place. Decorate at will if you have some scraps of pastry left and brush with beaten egg. Place in the oven for 40 minutes.

When you remove it, let it rest for a couple of minutes. Turn it out and reverse it. Serve at once. A cake tin with a collapsible bottom could facilitate matters.

Courgette soufflé

I made my favourite soufflé with courgettes last week and it was so good
I made another a few days later. It has all the glory of a cheese soufflé, with the
added bonus of the delicate courgette flavour and the charming pale-green colour
to boot. It is extremely easy to make and works a treat, as do all soufflés if you are
firm with them. This one is made in a dish with a 1 litre (1³/₄ pint) capacity, and will
be sufficient for two greedy people as a main course or three at a pinch.

SERVES 2 – 3

50g (2 oz) butter
dried breadcrumbs
450g (1 lb) courgettes, topped
and tailed
salt

40g (1½ oz) plain flour (2 level tablespoons)
150ml (¼ pint) milk, warmed
freshly ground pepper
50g (2 oz) freshly grated gruyère cheese
2 whole eggs, separated

Preheat the oven to 220°C/425°F/Gas 7.

Butter your soufflé dish lavishly with half the butter, throw in a
spoonful of fine dried breadcrumbs, rotate the dish until the sides and
bottom are coated with crumbs then empty any surplus into the rub-
bish bin. I keep a plastic bag in the boiler cupboard into which I put
any old bits of leftover bread, crusts and all; they will dry nicely and
when needed can be easily made into the finest of breadcrumbs in a
processor or blender, then stored in a jar.

Onward – slice the courgettes into thin rounds, sprinkle with a
little salt, mix together and leave to drain in a sieve for about an hour.
Squeeze as much moisture as you can out of them, then steam over
boiling water until quite soft.

Make a thick béchamel sauce from the rest of the butter melted
in a little saucepan, add the flour, stir well until thoroughly mixed,
then add the warmed milk little by little. Season with a good deal of
freshly ground pepper but hold the salt as yet. Sieve the courgettes
(use a mouli) into the béchamel, stir in the grated cheese until all is
smooth and melted, then off the fire add the well-beaten egg yolks.

Transfer to a large bowl able to receive the beaten egg whites, leave to cool.

Beat the 4 egg whites until stiff enough to make peaks, then carefully fold into the courgette mixture with a metal spoon, tasting for salt before completion: you may not need any. Pour the mixture into the dish, sprinkle the top with cheese, stand the dish in a baking tin filled with as much water as possible, then place in the middle of the preheated oven for exactly 30 minutes.

Hey presto, a triumph. If you want to make larger quantities, just double everything and use two soufflé dishes rather than one.

Boeuf à la Mode

During some really hot weather, I thought to make the cold, jellied version of that great dish of beef which uses silverside, top rump or topside. I think the fresh silverside or rump is best, as the topside tends to get shreddy.

SERVES 8–10

1.5–1.75kg (3–4 lb) fresh silverside (or the others)

100g (4 oz) fat pork back or bacon

1 large onion, chopped

olive oil

50ml (2 fluid oz) brandy

300ml (½ pint) red wine

4 pig's trotters

2 crushed cloves of garlic

bouquet of bay leaves, thyme and parsley

900g (2 lb) carrots

beef or veal stock

salt

freshly ground black pepper

1 dessertspoon sugar

chopped parsley

Preheat the oven to 140°C/275°F/Gas 1.

The meat is best made into a longish roll, and if you have a kind butcher ask him to lard it with the pork fat; otherwise cut the fat into strips and insert lengthwise into the meat with a larding needle or by making long stab wounds and pushing the fat in with a skewer. This prevents the meat getting dry within.

Brown the beef with the onion in a little oil, transfer to a large casserole, heat the brandy in the used pan, scraping any bits into it, set on fire and pour flaming over the beef. Add the wine, tuck the trotters round the meat with the garlic and the bouquet of herbs tied in a bunch, plus 225g (8 oz) of the carrots, sliced. Cover with beef stock. (If you must use cubes use 'Just Bouillon' made by Kallo, which have no artificial additives.)

Bring to simmering point on top of the stove, cover with foil and the lid and place in the lower part of the preheated oven for four to five hours, depending on the size of the joint; a 1.5kg (3 lb) piece should be done after four hours. It must be very tender when pierced.

Remove the meat from the casserole and reserve wrapped in foil to keep moist. Remove the pig's trotters, which can be used for *Pieds de Porc Panés* (bread-crumbed and grilled). Strain the stock and season to taste. When cool put into the refrigerator to chill, then you can clear all the fat off with ease.

Cook the rest of the carrots, sliced diagonally for charm, in more beef stock with a dessertspoon of sugar. Strain and cool. The jellied stock must now be melted but not at all hot, so when you see that it is half liquid turn the heat off and stir until no globules remain. Place the de-stringed meat into a deep oval dish in which you have made a dainty arrangement with the carrots at the bottom, pour the melted stock over all; it should cover the meat. Return to the refrigerator to chill until set.

When ready to serve, turn out on to a suitable oval platter and sprinkle with a little chopped parsley. It looks magnificent with the pattern of carrots shining through the dark amber jelly which will be stiff as cheese. Cut into slices and serve with a salad. If you must have a hot potato put it on another plate or it will damage the jelly.

Cardamom steamed salmon on bean salad

Here is a lovely way to give farmed salmon an exotic flavour.

SERVES 2

225g (8 oz) salmon fillet
1 courgette, sliced
1 tablespoon butter

For fish seasoning:

3 tablespoons lemon juice
6 tablespoons olive oil
1 ½ teaspoons ground cardamom

1 teaspoon ground star anise
½ teaspoon freshly ground black
pepper

For the salad:

225g (8 oz) green beans
225g (8 oz) lettuce hearts

3 tablespoons shredded basil
1 tablespoon lemon balm or mint

Skin the salmon and chop into cubes. Combine the fish seasoning ingredients and mix half of this mixture with the salmon. Reserve the other half for the salad. Sauté the courgette slices in the butter for 2–3 minutes, add the fish mixture, cover and steam over a low heat for 2 minutes. Make sure the fish is not overcooked.

Cut the beans into 7.5cm (3 inch) strips and boil in another pan. When still hot, mix the lettuce hearts with the beans, most of the basil and the lemon balm or mint. Top with the salmon, pour over the remaining fish seasoning and decorate with some more shredded basil. A good little supper dish.

PLATE ONE

Asparagus and Smoked Salmon Tarts

See page 21

PLATE TWO
Turkey Loaf
See page 28

PLATE THREE

Sea Bass with Black Olives

See page 34

Upside-down Pear Pudding
See page 46

PLATE FIVE
Lobster Risotto
See page 52

PLATE SIX

Tomato Aspic Ring

See page 54

PLATE SEVEN
Cardamom Steamed Salmon on Bean Salad
See page 64

PLATE EIGHT

White Peaches in Redcurrant Syrup

See page 80

Gigot of monkfish

Visitors to Reggio nell'Emilia in Italy will be surprised to discover that
the city's most famous saint, Bishop Prosper, is commemorated not by the great
cathedral but by the little church of San Prospero, tucked away behind it in the market
square. Saint Prosper, who died on 25 June in the year 466, built the church outside the
walls of Reggio and directed that he should be buried there. But the people of Reggio
made him their patron saint and in the year 703 his remains were moved to their
present resting-place inside the city walls. He may well be the patron of prosperity,
if you need it, but in fact he gave away all his possessions to the poor. A very
nice and gentle saint. Twenty-ninth June is the feast of Peter and Paul and
I think a fine fish dish is appropriate. I was once given a great deal of
cream by my neighbour, Caroline Spencer, and thought this up to use
some of it. You can get jars of mushrooms in large supermarkets.

SERVES 4–6

tailpiece of monkfish, 0.5–1.5kg (1–3 lb)
2 plump cloves garlic, cut into fine slivers
Maldon salt and freshly ground black
pepper
olive oil
120ml (4 fluid oz) dry vermouth or
Chambéry, warmed

275g (10 oz) preserved wild mushrooms
in oil
175ml (6 fluid oz) thick cream
1 tbsp chopped parsley
1 tbsp chopped tarragon
lemon juice

Preheat the oven to 220°C/425°F/Gas 7.

Ask the fishmonger to remove the membrane from the fish or
do it yourself. Place the fish in a suitable oven-proof dish. Insert the
slivers of garlic with a sharp knife. Season well with Maldon salt and
freshly ground pepper and anoint with olive oil. Cover and place in
the preheated oven for 15 minutes, then turn the heat down to
180°C/350°F/Gas 4. Add the warmed vermouth or Chambéry, and
cook for a further 30 minutes, basting occasionally.

When the fish is just about done, add the mushrooms, cream,
parsley and tarragon, adjust the seasoning and add a little lemon juice

to taste. Stir everything together, basting the fish, and return to a hot oven, 220°C/425°F/Gas 7, for 5 minutes.

Serve in the cooking dish with plain new potatoes, and I added samphire, but hot cucumber would be good.

Coley mayonnaise

I made a very good fish mayonnaise with that unfashionable fish, the coley. It is a marvellous fish, otherwise known as saithe or coal fish, but people in our dear and pleasant land disdain it as cat food because of its rather unattractive greyish colour when raw; do not let this depress you in the least, the flesh will become white when cooked and is firm in texture, falling into good-sized flakes. It is also far cheaper than the once humble cod which now has risen to wild pretensions.

SERVES 6

900g (2 lb) of fresh coley
sea salt
peppercorns
bay leaf

fennel seeds
juice of ½ lemon
chopped dill

For the mayonnaise:

2 egg yolks
½ teaspoon dry mustard
a pinch of salt
300ml (½ pint) olive oil, not too

strong-tasting
juice of ½ lemon
1 dessertspoon Pernod

Get the thick end of the coley, as it makes better flakes. Fill a frying pan or saucepan with enough water to cover the fish. Add sea salt, peppercorns, bay leaf and about a teaspoon of crushed fennel seeds; also squeeze half a lemon into the pan. Lay the fish in the water, bring to simmering point and poach gently for about 15–20 minutes, depending on its thickness. It is ready when you can prise the flesh from the skin and it has become white right though.

Make the mayonnaise. Put the egg yolks, mustard powder and salt in a bowl and beat them together. Add the oil drop by drop, whisking in each drop before adding the next until it starts to emulsify and thicken, then you can add the oil in a steady stream. Add half the lemon juice at half-time, the other half and the Pernod at the end, mixing in well.

When the fish is cool enough to handle, remove the skin, bones and any tough membrane from the flank. Arrange the fish in a flat dish in one layer of good-sized flakes. Coat the fish with the mayonnaise, sprinkle with chopped dill and serve with lovely little new potatoes (hot or cold) and a green bean salad. If you hate Pernod don't use it, the lemon will suffice, but the Pernod does go very well with the fish.

Turkey tonnato

Nice weather screams for delicious cold food that has been prepared ahead in the cool of the morning. Using turkey rather than traditional veal, and thus upsetting no one, this makes a very satisfactory substitute for *Vitello tonnato* which is one of the loveliest dishes, good for first or second courses and excellent in large quantities for parties or buffets. I used one of those curious-looking amputated turkey breasts from the supermarket which provides plenty of meat.

SERVES 6

1 whole turkey breast on the bone

1 carrot

1 stick celery

1 onion

bay leaf

parsley, about 6 sprigs

1 dessertspoon salt

300ml (½ pint) mayonnaise (see page 66 but omit Pernod)

For the sauce:

1 x 200g (7 oz) tin of tuna in olive oil, Italian preferably

5 anchovy fillets

300ml (½ pint) olive oil

3 tablespoons lemon juice

3 tablespoons capers

For the garnish:

olives

capers

radishes

Put the turkey breast, carrot, celery, onion, bay leaf and about six sprigs of parsley into a saucepan just large enough to contain them. Add enough water to cover the breast and about a dessertspoon of salt. Bring to the boil, then turn down the heat to barely simmering and poach for about quarter of an hour per pound, or until the flesh is tender when pierced and produces no trace of pink in its juices. Remove from the heat and let it cool in the liquid: this will keep it nice and moist.

Prepare the mayonnaise. Please make your own: it is no trouble as long as the ingredients are all at room temperature. Anything chilled from the refrigerator will kill it dead. Use two egg yolks, half a pint of good olive oil and about two tablespoons of lemon juice. You can use an electric beater if you must but it is better by hand, and I find it a soothing and joyful task. See p. 67 for method.

For the sauce, put the tuna, anchovies, olive oil, lemon juice and capers into a blender and whizz into a purée, then fold it carefully into the mayonnaise. Check the seasoning. Carve the cooled turkey breast into nice slices. Smear the bottom of your chosen dish or plate with some of the tuna mayonnaise. Arrange the turkey slices in a single layer, then spread liberally with the sauce; continue thus until you have used up all the slices, leaving enough sauce to cover the last layer generously. Cover the whole thing with cling-film and refrigerate for 24 hours to let the flavours sink in.

When ready to serve, decorate with olives, capers and radishes. A good potato salad and maybe some sliced tomatoes would be a suitable accompaniment.

Summer Accompaniments

Couscous salad

**You can make this salad the day before if it's any help.
It is particularly good served with the *Spiced Chicken* on page 58.**

SERVES 4–6

40g (1½ oz) butter
350ml (12 fluid oz) chicken stock
250g (9 oz) couscous
100g (4 oz) seedless raisins
1 bunch spring onions
75g (3 oz) sunflower seeds (optional)
50ml (2 fluid oz) lemon juice

½ teaspoon paprika
120ml (4 fluid oz) olive oil, warmed
1 teaspoon good salt
freshly ground black pepper
4–5 tablespoons fresh herbs, finely
chopped (parsley, chives, tarragon
or basil)

Melt the butter in a large pan, add the stock and bring to the boil. Stir in the couscous. Remove from the heat and let it stand covered for 10–12 minutes. Break up any lumps with a fork and transfer to a beautiful bowl. The grains should have absorbed all the liquid. Add the raisins, chopped spring onions and sunflower seeds, mixing all together.

Make a dressing for the couscous by blending all the rest of the ingredients together. Pour over the salad, and lightly toss it about, adding more salt, pepper and paprika, if needed, to suit your taste. You could also have a side dish of kidney beans and finely chopped spring onions dressed with a vinaigrette – it looks pretty and goes very well.

Puréed basil potatoes

I trust you have enormous quantities of basil sprouting from your window boxes or gardens during the summer, for here is the most delicious form of puréed potatoes I have ever had. It comes from my friend Suzie Booth.

SERVES 6–8

900g (2 lb) potatoes (Maris Piper, Belle de Fontenay, Binges or King Edward)
300ml (½ pint) single cream

75g (3 oz) basil leaves
150ml (¼ pint) olive oil
salt and freshly ground black pepper

Boil the potatoes in their skins until just cooked. Simmering rather than wild boiling is best to avoid bursting skins. Turn out into the sink, then peel as soon as manageable. Purée through a mouli into a warmed pot or casserole. Add the cream, slightly heated. Keep the potatoes hot over a saucepan of boiling water. Place the basil leaves and the olive oil in a blender or processor and whizz into a green sludge. Beat the sludge into the potatoes and season with good salt and a lavish amount of freshly ground black pepper.

This produces a wonderful mound of pale-green potatoes with a scent of heaven. Excellent with pale-pink lamb, red beef, fish or practically anything.

Melazane a funghetti

The aubergines in the market look particularly beautiful in the summer, glossy and plump. What a lovely vegetable they are, but very few people seem to use them in their own right. They either get stuffed, baked with cheese and tomato sauce or used for moussaka and ratatouille; all very good, but they can be used as a separate vegetable and make a very good accompaniment to any meat or chicken dish; I think they go perfectly with lamb. The Italians simply sauté them in olive oil.

SERVES 6—8

4 perfect aubergines
150ml (¼ pint) good olive oil
3 plump cloves of garlic

salt
freshly ground pepper
chopped parsley

Cut the aubergines into cubes of about 1cm (½ inch). Put them into a large sieve or colander, sprinkle them with a little salt, then turn them over and over to distribute it. Leave to drain in the sink for an hour or so. Squeeze them to remove moisture and roll them in a tea-towel.

Heat the olive oil in a large frying pan, put in the aubergines and cook over a gentle heat, turning them over now and then until they are soft, about 20 minutes. Halfway through, add the garlic chopped finely. When ready, season to your taste (remember the aubergines have already been salted); they can take quite a lot of freshly ground pepper. Transfer to a warmed dish and sprinkle with chopped parsley.

This is also excellent cold as a salad. The term 'funghetti' in this case has nothing to do with mushrooms, it is merely a method of cooking the vegetables with their skins on.

Potatoes Ruspoli

A few years ago I visited Tuscany, in the midst of the Chianti Classico country
where I stayed with my old *Candid Camera* mate Jonathan Routh and his wife Shelagh.
While we all know quite a bit about Tuscan food by now, we may forget the wonderful
natural produce out there: the gorgeous gnarled tomatoes; the buffalo mozzarella,
figs, pears, peppers and cheeses which really taste; whole, stuffed, roasted pigs
in the market; grilled pigeons of melting tenderness and vast veal chops
all cooked on the charcoal fires.
While we were there, I had a very good Italian lunch at the house of Julio Ruspoli
who produces a very excellent Chianti Classico red which we imbibed. The lunch was
delicious but the dish that caught my fancy was an unusual potato mixture.

SERVES 4—6

750g (1½ lb) potatoes
2 large yellow pimentos
2 good-sized onions
3 tablespoons olive oil

300ml (½ pint) good stock, warmed
salt
freshly ground pepper
chopped parsley

Use new or waxy potatoes that will not dwindle into a mush. Scrub or
scrape them and cut into smallish chunks. De-seed the pimentos, cut
away the pith and slice fairly thickly into diamond shapes. Chop up the
onions and fry gently in the olive oil until soft. Add the potatoes and
the pimentos, mix well with the onions, then pour in half the warmed
stock. Cook until tender, uncovered, adding more stock if necessary
(I used the full 300ml/½ pint).

   When ready, season with salt and freshly ground pepper and
sprinkle with a good handful of chopped parsley. Serve with any meat,
poultry or fish dish. It is also very good when cold as a salad.

Ricotta and beetroot salad

This variation on the mozzarella and tomato salad was given to me by
a man who had just arrived from Sardinia, so I am not quite sure where its true
locale is. It has a beautiful appearance, though I know beetroot is anathema
to some poor folk.

SERVES 4

225g (8 oz) fresh ricotta
225g (8 oz) cooked beetroots
fresh mint, parsley and chives

For the vinaigrette:

red wine vinegar   olive oil
lemon juice   salt and freshly ground pepper

Buy fresh firm ricotta from an Italian delicatessen so it is possible to
slice neatly, and so do. Slice the beetroots and interleave with the
ricotta on a dainty shallow dish. Make the vinaigrette with red wine
vinegar, a squeeze or so of lemon juice and five times as much fruity
olive oil; add salt and freshly ground pepper to taste. Pour liberally
over the salad and leave for at least an hour before eating. Sprinkle
with a good chopping of mint, parsley or chives or all three mixed
together.

An exciting titbit to give with drinks is fried sage leaves – very
good news for anyone who grows it, as it is always so prolific. Dip
little branches of sage into well-seasoned flour, then into a well-
beaten whole egg. Fry in sizzling sunflower oil until crisp and golden,
drain and eat at once.

Spinach and potato timbales

The following jolly little creatures are delicious with cold ham or other meats and chicken, or they can be served on their own with a good Italian tomato sauce.

SERVES 4

1 onion, finely chopped
25g (1 oz) butter
250g (9 oz) fresh spinach, washed
450g (1 lb) potatoes, cooked and mashed
225g (8 oz) mascarpone cheese

100g (4 oz) plain flour
good pinch freshly grated nutmeg
salt
freshly ground pepper
2 size 3 eggs, beaten

Preheat the oven to 180°C/350°F/Gas 4. Fry the onion in a little butter until soft. Blanch the spinach in boiling water for 1 minute. Drain and rinse in cold water before squeezing in a clean tea-towel to remove excess liquid. Chop the spinach and mix with the onion, butter, mashed potato, cheese, flour and nutmeg. Season to taste, then bind with the beaten eggs. Divide the mixture between four oven-proof moulds and cover loosely with oiled foil. Place in a large roasting tin, then add enough water to reach halfway up the sides of the moulds. Cook in the oven for 25–30 minutes. Turn out and serve at once.

Bob Schultz's meatballs

During a lovely after-Sunday-Mass drink with the splendid Bob Schultz, the Aussie of *haute couture* in the days when fashion was fashion, he gave me an interesting method for making meatballs; quite different and much stronger than the usual ones associated with spaghetti.

SERVES 6—8

4 slices stale white bread – good-quality milk

450g (1 lb) good lean beef mince

2 good handfuls parsley

1 tablespoon grated lemon zest

1 tablespoon grated fresh ginger root

2 crushed garlic cloves

75g (3 oz) of freshly grated Parmesan cheese

2 medium eggs, beaten

salt

freshly ground pepper

plain flour or fine toasted breadcrumbs

olive oil

I found this quantity made 16 meatballs, the size of golf balls, which I flattened a bit for easier frying. They looked more like mini-burgers. Soak the slices of bread in milk; when saturated squeeze the milk out and add to the mince in a bowl. Chop the parsley, including the stalks for flavour. Add the parsley, lemon zest, ginger, garlic, Parmesan cheese and the two eggs to the beef and bread. Season with freshly ground pepper and a little salt, remembering the cheese is quite salty.

Mix all the ingredients very thoroughly; I find hands the best implement. Form into golf-ball-size balls. Roll in the flour or breadcrumbs (not that terrible stuff bought in packets – make your own); I rolled mine in a mixture of both, which produced a nice, crisp exterior.

Heat some olive oil in a large frying pan and cook the little creatures until browned all over. It is up to you whether you want them rare or not. Very good with any nice vegetables, or rice and a tomato salad. If you made them on a tiny scale they would be a delicious titbit with drinks.

Summer Desserts

Amaretti and strawberry terrine

I was once on some crazy food quiz with Sophie Grigson,
which reminded me of a really easy and heavenly pudding she gave us in
London's *Evening Standard* newspaper.

SERVES 8–10

600ml (1 pint) double cream

2 teaspoons rose water

25g (1 oz) caster sugar

25g (1 oz) vanilla sugar

65g (2½ oz) amaretti biscuits, crushed

225g (8 oz) strawberries, hulled and quartered

For the raspberry sauce:

275g (10 oz) raspberries

lemon juice

icing sugar to sweeten

Whip the cream with the rose water until just stiff, and fold in the sugars (if you haven't got vanilla sugar or rose water, never mind, just use 50g (2 oz) of sugar with a few drops of real vanilla essence). Add the crushed amaretti, mix well.

Line a 1.5 litre (2½ pint) loaf tin with silver foil. Spread half the cream mixture on the base of the tin. Cover with the strawberries, pressing them gently into the cream. Cover with the rest of the mixture, smoothing it lightly into place. Cover with foil and chill in the refrigerator for six hours or overnight.

Crush the raspberries through a sieve (or mouli), reserving just a few for decoration later, then add a dash of lemon juice and just enough sugar to sweeten a touch, but keep it tartish.

Just before serving, turn the terrine out onto a dainty dish, ease off the foil, decorate with a few raspberries or strawberries and pour the sauce around it, like the pool of blood in which 'the bravest 'Truscans lay'.

Lemon syllabub with red fruits

Now for a beautiful summer's pudding.

SERVES 4

For the lemon syllabub:

120ml (4 fluid oz) dry white wine

50ml (2 fluid oz) brandy

1 teaspoon grated lemon rind

juice of 1 lemon

1 tablespoon clear honey

300ml (½ pint) double cream

pinch of freshly grated nutmeg

For the red fruits:

1 punnet each of strawberries, raspberries, blackberries and redcurrants

120ml (4 fluid oz) crème de cassis

75g (3 oz) caster sugar

1 tablespoon lemon juice

To make the syllabub, place the first five ingredients in a china bowl and leave overnight for the flavours to mingle and develop. Next day, add the cream and nutmeg, and beat with a whisk until the syllabub holds its shape. (Be careful not to beat too much, otherwise it might curdle.) Pour into a glass bowl and refrigerate.

Prepare and clean the red fruits, quartering the strawberries. In another glass bowl, combine all the fruits gently with the cassis, sugar and lemon juice. Allow to macerate for about 3 hours, turning the fruits from time to time.

Serve both bowls together and let the folks choose and mix.

Almond cream with berries

When all the summer berries are at their peak, try this Italian pudding for a little change from cream with everything.

SERVES 6

450g (1 lb) cream cheese or ricotta
225g (8 oz) caster sugar
4 tablespoons ground almonds (fresh is best)

4 tablespoons orange or lemon liqueur
900g (2 lb) mixed strawberries, raspberries, redcurrants etc.

Beat the cheese and sugar until creamy in a processor or by hand, then gradually beat in the almonds and the liqueur. Place in a mound in the middle of a large dish and surround with prepared fruits. Maybe a few tiny mint leaves for decoration.

Almond meringues

I made some old-fashioned gooseberry fool the other day and, having no ratafias or macaroons, I made some meringues to accompany the fool. I was inspired to add almonds to the mixture.

4 egg whites
225g (8 oz) caster sugar

75g (3 oz) ground almonds
1 teaspoon almond essence (not flavouring)

Preheat the oven to 120°C/250°F/Gas ½.

Beat the egg whites until stiff, add half the sugar and beat again. Fold in the rest of the sugar, then the almonds and the essence. Cover two baking tins with non-stick baking parchment and spoon the meringue mixture in little blobs on to them. Place in the preheated oven for 1½ hours, changing tray positions at half-time. Allow to cool, then munch away.

White peaches in redcurrant syrup

Now for a beautiful seasonal pudding.

SERVES 4

4 ripe peaches, preferably fragrant
white peaches

2 tablespoons water

100g (4 oz) sugar (measurewise)

350g (12 oz) fresh redcurrants

4 fresh mint leaves

If by some heaven-sent chance you can lay your hands on those wonderful garden-wall white peaches, they are the best; otherwise use any you can buy in the market.

In a small saucepan, heat the water and the sugar over a medium heat until the sugar is completely dissolved.

Rinse the redcurrants well, then pick them over, discarding the tough stems; don't worry about the small stems attached to the fruit. Place the currants in the middle of a clean kitchen towel or some layers of butter-muslin. Wrap the sides of the towel round the fruit and twist the ends. Hold over a bowl and continue twisting and turning to squeeze as much juice as possible out of the fruit. Add three-quarters of the sugar syrup to the currant juice and taste, adding more if desired.

Place the peaches in boiling water for 30 seconds, remove and peel when cool enough. Halve and stone the peaches. Arrange in a glass dish, pour the redcurrant juice over them, cover with cling-film and leave to marinate overnight in the refrigerator. Serve with a mint leaf and some good vanilla ice-cream. Divine.

Soft meringues with egg custard

This is a receipt for creamy meringues filled with egg custard, which were made by the nuns in Portugal for the feast of the Assumption of the Blessed Virgin Mary, a ladies' feast to be celebrated with sweet delicacies, according to Elisabeth Luard.

.... MAKES 70 MERINGUES ....

For the custard:

350g (12 oz) sugar
450ml (1 pint) water
1 curl of lemon peel

175g (6 oz) rice flour
9 egg yolks

For the meringues:

750g (1¾ lb) caster sugar
450ml (¾ pint) water
9 egg whites

1 tablespoon lemon juice
½ teaspoon salt

....

First the custard. Put the sugar and 300ml (½ pint) of the water in a saucepan, and bring to the boil with the lemon peel, stirring until it dissolves into a syrup. Remove the peel and boil the syrup until it reaches hard-ball stage, 120°C/246°F on a sugar thermometer when a drop hardens on an icy saucer.

Meanwhile mix the rice flour with the remaining water. Whisk the egg yolks until light and frothy. Pour the boiling syrup in a thin stream into the egg yolks, whisking assiduously as you pour. Stir in the rice flour mix. Return all to a gentle heat and simmer very, very gently, stirring all the time with a wooden spoon until the custard holds the trace of the spoon. Make sure it doesn't catch on the base of the pan. Pour into a bowl, cover with cling-film and allow to cool. This can all be done the day before if you are feeling exhausted.

For the meringues, preheat the oven to 150°C/300°F/Gas 2.

Dissolve the sugar in the water, then boil steadily until it reaches the soft-ball stage, 112°C/236°F on the sugar thermometer or making a soft ball when dripped onto an icy saucer. Whisk the egg whites with the lemon juice and salt until they are stiff. Pour in the boiling syrup, whisking away as with the custard. Go on whisking until it is stiff and shining white.

Line baking trays with baking parchment (such a godsend for meringues). Drop on rounded tablespoons of the egg whites and bake for 30 minutes. Leave them in the turned-off oven for an hour to dry out.

Sandwich the meringues together with the custard. Delicious with iced fruit drinks or iced coffee. This makes about six dozen meringues, suitable for a party, but of course you can cut the quantities to suit your needs.

Autumn

starters

Duck liver pâté with orange relish
Minestrone alla Milanese
Pumpkin soup

Cake au jambon
Watercress mousse with red pepper sauce
Eggs poached in red wine

main courses

Hare à la Royale
Coq au vin
Beef stew with red wine and brandy
Pheasant with celery
Casserole of wild rabbit with cream and
tarragon

Lamb sweetbreads
Boeuf à la mode Caroline
Baked egg and spinach pie with pancetta
Autumn braised leg of lamb
Alaskan hotpot
Southern Italian fried chicken

accompaniments

Celeriac purée
Roast tomatoes

Garlic mushrooms
Céleri rémoulade

desserts

Pumpkin cheesecake
Charlotte clementines
Sudden death

Floreat Etona
Patrick's bread and butter pudding

Autumn Starters

Duck liver pâté with orange relish

The glorious Thane Prince – food writer on the *Saturday Telegraph* – has provided me with this delectable receipt.

························ SERVES 4 ························

2 tablespoons olive oil
2 large shallots, finely chopped
1 large clove garlic, peeled and crushed
400g (14 oz) fresh duck livers
65g (2½ oz) butter

150ml (¼ pint) double cream
grated zest of a well-scrubbed orange
salt
freshly ground black pepper
2 tablespoons brandy

For the orange relish:

1 tablespoon oil
1 shallot, peeled and chopped
4 tablespoons good orange marmalade
juice of 1 orange

juice and zest of 1 lemon
salt
Tabasco

Heat the oil in a heavy frying pan. Cook the shallots until soft but not browned, then add the garlic and cook for a further minute. Trim the livers and add to the pan. Cook over a moderate heat, turning at intervals until almost cooked through but still pink inside. Add the butter, cream, orange zest and plenty of salt and freshly ground black pepper.

Simmer for a further minute. Tip the contents of the pan into a blender, add the brandy and whizz until smooth. Spoon into a suitable pâté dish (I use a soufflé one), cover and chill overnight or at least six hours.

To make the relish, heat the oil in a small saucepan and fry the shallot until soft. Add the marmalade, orange juice, lemon juice and zest, cooking and stirring until you have a well-amalgamated sauce. Season to taste with salt and Tabasco, simmer for 1–2 minutes, then cool.

Serve the pâté with hot brown toast or a crusty baguette and the orange relish on the side.

Minestrone alla Milanese

Now, how about the great life-giving soup of Italy, a thick soup of many vegetables with many different versions, sometimes including rice, sometimes pasta? Here is the one favoured in Milan.

SERVES 8

50g (2 oz) pancetta (unsmoked streaky bacon)

50g (2 oz) unsalted butter

3 onions, sliced

4 carrots, diced

2 celery sticks, diced

150g (5 oz) borlotti beans, soaked overnight

2 medium courgettes, diced

100g (4 oz) French beans, trimmed and diced

100g (4 oz) shelled peas

200g (7 oz) savoy cabbage, sliced

2l (3½ pints) meat stock

350g (12 oz) potatoes, peeled and halved

225g (8 oz) fresh or tinned tomatoes

salt and freshly ground pepper

175g (6 oz) Italian rice

75g (3 oz) freshly grated Parmesan cheese

Try to buy the real pancetta: it has a fine, distinctive flavour. Melt the butter in a large, heavy saucepan or earthenware pot. Cook the pancetta and onion gently for five minutes, then add the carrots and celery. After three minutes, add the borlotti beans, stir for a further five minutes, then in go the courgettes, French beans and shelled peas.

After a further five minutes, stir in the cabbage until it is coated with the fat. Pour in the stock, add the potatoes, tomatoes, salt and freshly ground pepper to taste. Bring the soup to the boil, reduce to a very slow simmer, cover and cook for about three hours.

If the potatoes need it, take them out, mash them and return to the soup. Check the seasoning. Add the rice and cook until *al dente* (about 12 minutes, but test). Stir in four tablespoons of the Parmesan cheese and hand round the remainder separately.

The *Minestrone alla Genovese* has a large tablespoon of pesto sauce added before serving.

Pumpkin soup

On the coast of Coromandel
Where the early pumpkins blow,
In the middle of the woods,
Lived the Yonghy-Bonghy-Bó.

I can't remember if the Yonghy-Bonghy-Bó made any use of the pumpkins, but I have been to pumpkin heaven in a little village past Arundel called Slindon where they grow an incredible variety of squashes and pumpkins. Pile upon pile of them, gleaming yellows, oranges, greens and cream – a wonderful sight to be seen.

SERVES 10

450g (1 lb) peeled and seeded pumpkin
10 spring onions
50g (2 oz) butter
350g (12 oz) potatoes
1 x 400g (14 oz) tin chopped tomatoes

1.2 litres (2 pints) good stock
salt
freshly ground black pepper
150ml (¼ pint) single cream
a handful of chopped parsley

Cut the pumpkin into small dice and chop the spring onions, using only the white parts. Melt the butter in a large soup saucepan, add the pumpkin and the onions and sweat over a low heat for about five minutes. Meanwhile, peel and slice the potatoes, add them to the pan and cook for a further few minutes. Pour in the tomatoes and the stock, mix, then season to taste with the salt and freshly ground black pepper. Bring to the boil, then lower the heat and simmer very gently for 1 hour.

Remove from the heat, and cool slightly before liquidising in a blender of some sort, or pass it through a sieve. Return the soup to the rinsed-out pan, stir in the cream and adjust the seasoning. Reheat the soup and sprinkle in the parsley before serving.

Put a bowl of fried croûtons on the table to add at will. The soup is a marvellous colour and, if wished, can be served chilled with a blob of sour cream and chopped chives to enhance it. This amount is ample for ten people.

Cake au jambon

Now for something entirely different – a mixture of a soufflé and a cake given to me by my neighbour Caroline Spencer. This is a Swiss receipt, I believe, and very good as a supper dish or a first course.

SERVES 4

50g (2 oz) flaked almonds or split pistachio nuts

100g (4 oz) butter

2 tablespoons oil – olive, corn, walnut or hazel

3 tablespoons sour cream or crème fraîche

3 egg yolks

big handful of parsley and basil

salt and freshly ground pepper

50g (2 oz) fresh grated Parmesan

50g (2 oz) fresh grated gruyère

175g (6 oz) good ham, finely diced

4 egg whites

150g (5 oz) self-raising flour

Preheat the oven to 190°C/375°F/Gas 5.

Lavishly butter our old friend the loaf tin. Sprinkle the nuts on the base and round the sides, if so desired. Into a processor place the butter, oil, cream, egg yolks, herbs, a lot of freshly ground pepper and a pinch of salt. Whizz into a purée, then turn into a bowl. Stir in the cheeses and the ham.

Whip the whites of egg stiffly; add a few spoonfuls to the mixture, then sift in the flour; mix thoroughly, adjust the seasoning – maybe a touch of Tabasco or cayenne? Fold in the rest of the whites, and pour into the loaf tin. Bake on an oven tray for 30 minutes.

When ready, run a knife around the inside of the tin and turn out to reveal the crunchy-nut bottom. Serve with a spicy tomato sauce with a helping of Dijon mustard stirred into it. Best hot, but also good cold.

Watercress mousse with red pepper sauce

Sally Bruce-Gardyne, widow of Jock Bruce-Gardyne, a very brave and splendid man and much-missed contributor to the *Spectator*, sent me a cookbook published in aid of St John Ambulance. Entitled *Lincolnshire Cookery Book*, it is a collection of receipts gathered from people of all ages from around the county. It costs a very reasonable £5.50 including postage and can be obtained from St John Ambulance HQ, 268 High Street, Lincoln LN2 1JG. Here is an excellent autumn starter from the book. Serve it with some hot garlic bread.

SERVES 4

For the watercress mousse:

1 tablespoon lemon juice	200g (8 oz) low-fat cream cheese
2 teaspoons powdered gelatine	4 tablespoons milk
75g (3 oz) watercress	salt and freshly ground pepper
3 spring onions	a few sprigs of watercress

For the red pepper sauce:

2 sweet red peppers	1 level teaspoon olive oil
½ clove of garlic	1 tablespoon lemon juice
1 level teaspoon of caster sugar	

Oil four ramekin dishes. For the mousse, put 1 tablespoon of cold water and the lemon juice into a cup and sprinkle with the gelatine.

Leave to soften for 5 minutes, then stand the cup in hot water until the gelatine dissolves and becomes clear. (Never let it boil.) Chop the watercress and spring onions in a food processor or what you will, add the cream cheese and milk, mix well and season. Add the gelatine mixture and give another whizz. Pour all this into the ramekins and leave for 2 hours in the refrigerator to set.

For the sauce, grill the peppers for 15–20 minutes, turning as the skin blackens and chars. Place in a plastic bag to cool, then peel off the skin, remove the core and seeds but retain quarter of the skin for garnish. Crush the garlic, then place in the food processor, together with the pepper flesh and sugar. Whizz until smooth, then add the olive oil and lemon juice.

To serve, turn out the mousses (surround the ramekins with boiling water for a moment). Place on separate plates and spoon the sauce around them. Decorate with the odd sprig of watercress and the pepper skin cut into strips.

Eggs poached in red wine

I once went on a lovely barge trip in Burgundy. The food was sublime: one of the first courses was this splendid dish of eggs poached in wine. It makes a very good autumn starter and combines four typical Burgundian ingredients – red wine, mushrooms, bacon and onions.

SERVES 4

For the eggs:

1.5 litres (1¾ pints) red wine (Pinot Noir or the like)

600ml (1 pint) good chicken or veal stock

1 bouquet garni

6 black peppercorns

pinch of salt

8 very fresh eggs

50g (2 oz) butter

1 onion, 1 carrot and 1 celery stalk, all thinly sliced

1 clove of garlic, crushed

40g (1½ oz) butter kneaded with 20g (¾ oz) plain flour

pinch of sugar (optional)

chopped fresh parsley

For the garnish:

knob of butter

150g (5 oz) bacon lardons, blanched

100g (4 oz) mushrooms, quartered

16–20 baby onions or shallots, peeled

For the croûtes:

oil

knob of butter

4 oval slices cut from a French loaf

Put the wine and stock in a deep, heavy frying pan with the bouquet garni, peppercorns and salt. Bring to the boil and poach the eggs, in two batches, for about 3 minutes until the yolks are firming but still soft. Carefully transfer the eggs on a slotted spoon to paper towels. Trim off any white strings and cover with a damp cloth.

Heat 25g (1 oz) of the butter in a saucepan, and briefly sauté the sliced onion, carrot, celery and crushed garlic. Add the poaching liquid with the herbs and seasonings, bring to the boil, then simmer for 15 minutes until the vegetables are tender. Boil the mixture until reduced by half. Then whisk enough of the kneaded flour and butter, bit by bit, into the boiling wine mixture to thicken the sauce to a light coating consistency. Simmer for 3 minutes and season to taste, adding a pinch of sugar if you wish. Strain, return to the pan and stir in the remaining butter a piece at a time.

For the garnish, heat the butter in a deep pan and sauté the bacon, mushrooms and onions or shallots until brown. Add the thickened sauce and simmer for 3 minutes.

Meanwhile, make the croûtes by heating some oil and butter in a pan and frying the slices of French bread.

Reheat the eggs in a bowl of hot water for 30 seconds, then drain on paper towels. Place the eggs on the croûtes, spoon the sauce and garnish over them, sprinkle with chopped parsley and serve at once.

Autumn
Main Courses

Hare à la Royale

A game dish fit for a king.

SERVES 4

50g (2 oz) butter
2 large rashers of bacon
1 hare, hung for 4 days, skinned and
drawn (retain liver and lungs)
20 cloves garlic, peeled
40 shallots, peeled
bouquet garni of 2 bay leaves

cloves
sprig of thyme
salt
freshly ground pepper
½ glass of wine vinegar
2 bottles of Burgundy
1 small glass of Cognac

Preheat the oven to 150°C/275–300°F/Gas 1–2.

Melt the butter in a heavy iron casserole, lay a rasher of bacon in the bottom, then the hare with the second rasher on top. Mince the garlic and the shallots and add to the hare with the bouquet garni and a few cloves to taste. Season with salt and freshly ground pepper, pour in the vinegar and one of the bottles of Burgundy. Cook over a slow heat for three hours (I prefer the oven).

Meanwhile, mince the hare's liver and lungs and any clots of blood and add them to the hare at the end of the first three-hour cooking, together with another half-bottle of Burgundy.

95

After another three hours the meat will have left the bones, which should be lifted out with two forks. Sprinkle the savoury, shapeless mass at the bottom of the pot with the Cognac, warm for five minutes and serve piping hot with bread and a spoon, a glass of your best Burgundy, that is all. *Lièvre à la Royale* is eaten with a spoon – and with reverence.

Coq au vin

Another classic wine dish is *Coq au Vin*, which used to be a good way to cook and tenderise a tough old cockerel. But, as we don't see many of them nowadays, we will use an ordinary roasting chicken and a bottle of inexpensive but sound red Burgundy or Beaujolais or Mâcon; take your pick.

SERVES 4–6

1.75kg (4 lb) roasting chicken with its liver

salt and pepper

75g (3 oz) butter

100g (4 oz) thick-cut streaky bacon, diced

12 button onions, peeled

40g (1½ oz) plain flour

4 tablespoons brandy

1 bottle red wine

225g (8 oz) button mushrooms

1 clove garlic, crushed

4 slices good white bread, cubed

frying oil

150ml (¼ pint) good chicken stock

Cut the chicken into eight pieces and season well with salt and pepper. Melt half the butter in a pan and fry the bacon and onions until well browned. Remove from the pan with a slotted spoon and keep at the ready.

Fry the chicken pieces in the same pan, adding more butter if necessary. When they are nice and brown on both sides, sprinkle them with the flour, turning and stirring well. Add the brandy, let it bubble; then the wine, mushrooms, garlic and the onions and bacon. Cover and simmer for 45 minutes.

Cut the chicken liver into a few strips, sauté gently for a minute

PLATE NINE

Cake au Jambon

See page 90

PLATE TEN
Pheasant with Celery
See page 98

PLATE ELEVEN

Autumn Braised Leg of Lamb

See page 105

PLATE TWELVE
Sudden Death
See page 115

PLATE THIRTEEN
Black Bean Soup
See page 123

PLATE FOURTEEN
Goat's Cheese Soufflé
See page 129

Steak and Kidney Pudding

See page 136

PLATE SIXTEEN

Suffolk Frozen Lemon Pudding

See page 151

in the remaining butter, keeping a pinkness, then push it with the fat through a little sieve; reserve it for the sauce. Fry the cubed bread in some oil until crisp and golden and drain on some kitchen paper. When the chicken is cooked transfer it to a nice hot serving dish with the bacon and vegetables, leaving the sauce in the pan.

Add the chicken stock to the wine sauce, turn up the heat and simmer steadily for about 20 minutes until the volume is reduced by half, add the sieved liver, bring to the boil then pour over the chicken. Sprinkle with the croûtons and serve at once. Noodles or rice are good with this dish and maybe a tomato salad on the side.

Beef stew with red wine and brandy

Autumn is a good time of the year to be thinking of aromatic and vinous stews simmering away for hours to delight the nostrils. Topside of beef seems to be usually recommended for stewing, but I am never very satisfied with the results. I find it tends to go stringy with its rather coarse grain. I think the unsalted silverside is more the thing, or, more expensively, top rump. I have cooked the following dish with the Bulgarian Reserve Melnik 1983 which I find very good both for the pot and the table.

SERVES 10–12

1.75kg (4 lb) piece silverside or top rump
pork or goose fat
2 large onions, sliced
5 largish carrots, halved lengthways
2 plump cloves garlic, slightly crushed
120ml (4 fluid oz) brandy

½ bottle of the Bulgarian Melnik
450g (1 lb) streaky salt pork, cut into cubes
2 pigs' trotters (split)
2 bay leaves, thyme and parsley
salt and freshly ground pepper

Have the meat tied into a neat shape for the heavy casserole you will be using. Melt about 50g (2 oz) of the fat in the pot, place the meat in the middle and surround it with the onions, carrots and garlic cloves. Cook gently for 15 minutes until the onions have taken on a little colour and you have browned the meat all over.

Pour in the brandy, let it bubble, then add the wine, the salt pork and the pigs' trotters, which will enrich the sauce. Tuck the herbs into the dish, season with a little salt and freshly ground pepper. Cover with foil and a well-fitting lid. Place in the lowest possible oven for about seven hours.

This will produce a delicious and tender piece of meat with a rather fatty sauce, so serve some plain boiled potatoes with it. If it is served cold, remove the vegetables immediately, and the fat when the jelly has set.

Pheasant with celery

I once had a pheasant cooked beautifully by an admirable barrister aptly named Richard Fowler. He served it in the traditional roast way and managed to keep it moist and succulent and, of course, it was well hung, so it had a real flavour. This is another method for a change.

SERVES 4

1 young, tender roasting pheasant
75g (3 oz) butter
50g (2 oz) streaky salt pork or unsmoked bacon, diced
salt and freshly ground pepper

120ml (4 fluid oz) dry white wine, heated
1 large head of celery
2 tablespoons olive oil
small glass of brandy, Armagnac or Calvados

To cook the pheasant it is best to have an oval casserole in which the bird just fits. Melt 25g (1 oz) of the butter in the pot, add the pork or bacon and start to sweat. Work the second 25g (1 oz) of butter with a little salt and freshly ground pepper and place it within the pheasant. When the fat from the pork starts melting, put the bird in on its side and let it cook gently until golden brown, before turning it over and adding the heated wine. Let the wine bubble for a few seconds, then turn the heat down very low, cover the pot and cook gently for 40 to 45 minutes, turning the bird over at half time.

Scrape the cleansed celery (try to get some good celery with taste, usually the dirtier the better), removing the strings from the outer stalks; trim off the leaves and cut into 1cm (½ inch) chunks. Melt the third 25g (1 oz) of butter and the olive oil in a large, heavy frying pan. Put in the celery and stir it around to coat with the fat, sprinkle a little salt over it, cover and let it simmer gently for 10 minutes. Take a tablespoon of the juices from the bird and stir into the celery, then cook for another five minutes.

Transfer to a fine, hot serving dish, large enough to hold the pheasant as well. Place the bird in the centre and, if convenient, carve for serving at this stage. Surround with the little bits of pork or bacon. Keep the dish warm and covered while you reduce the juices in the pot by boiling rapidly for a minute or two. Add the brandy or whatever and cook for a minute longer. Transfer to a hot sauce-boat and serve with the pheasant.

Celery goes very well with game birds, and this makes a handsome dish needing but a few little potatoes to accompany it.

Casserole of wild rabbit with cream and tarragon

I am exceedingly fond of rabbit and this is exceedingly good and simple.

SERVES 8

2 wild rabbits

salt and freshly ground black pepper

50g (2 oz) butter

olive oil

1 onion, finely chopped

1 leek, finely chopped

2 garlic cloves, crushed

2 litres (3½ pints) chicken stock

1 bunch tarragon

150ml (¼ pint) small carton double cream

Preheat the oven to 190°C/375°F/Gas 5.

Ask your friendly butcher to chop the rabbits into pieces, unless you are good at it yourself. Season them with salt and pepper. Heat the butter with a drop of oil until good and hot, and brown the rabbit pieces for about five minutes to seal the meat. When browned all over, transfer to a heavy casserole with a slotted spoon.

Lower the heat and add the onion to the pan with a little more oil if necessary. Cook for about five minutes, then add the leek and garlic and let them sweat for another five minutes or so. Using the slotted spoon, arrange the onion and leek around the meat in the casserole.

De-glaze the pan with a cup of the stock, scraping any little bits into the liquid. Pour into the casserole and add the rest of the stock. Remove the leaves from the tarragon and reserve. Tie the stalks together and insert into the rabbit pieces. Cover the casserole and cook for two hours in the oven.

Just before serving, remove the casserole from the oven, remove the bundle of tarragon stalks from within, stir in the cream and the leaves of tarragon, coarsely chopped. Mix well and adjust the seasoning. A squeeze of lemon juice does not come amiss. Serve with a creamy purée of celeriac and potatoes, using twice as much celeriac as potatoes (see page 109).

Lamb sweetbreads

I adore sweetbreads, which are not, despite the popular misconception, testicles, but the thymus gland, though I did once cook testicles in Benghazi due to early ignorance. But they were delicious in any case, so all was well.

SERVES 6

900g (2 lb) lamb sweetbreads
light veal or chicken stock or white wine
and water
2 carrots, sliced
1 onion, sliced
1 celery stick, sliced
streaky bacon slices

2 sprigs of parsley
salt and freshly ground pepper
100g (4 oz) butter
100g (4 oz) mushrooms, cut into
chunks
6 slices of French bread, cut open
100g (4 oz) thick cream

Soak the sweetbreads in salted water for at least an hour. Drain and place in a saucepan. Cover with the stock or a mixture of wine and water. Bring slowly to simmering point and cook for three minutes. Drain but reserve the cooking liquid. Rinse the sweetbreads in a bowl under cold running water. With your hands remove any fat and nasty little nodules and the thicker bits of membrane.

Place the sweetbreads between two plates or boards with a weight on top and chill (overnight if you wish). This will give them a uniform thickness.

Preheat the oven to 150°C/300°F/Gas 1–2.

Find a casserole which will just fit the sweetbreads in a single layer. Place the vegetables at the bottom, then a layer of streaky bacon, then the sweetbreads and then another layer of bacon. Cover with the reserved cooking liquid, add the parsley and season well. Bring to simmering point, then transfer, covered, to the preheated oven for 45 minutes.

For the last stage, you need two frying pans each with 50g (2 oz) of the butter melted in it. Fry the mushrooms just briefly in one, then remove with a slotted spoon to a separate plate. Next fry the slices of French bread, adding more butter as necessary.

At the same time, in the second pan, very gently sauté the sweetbreads on each side until they are palest gold. Add the mushrooms and 2–4 tablespoons of the cooking liquid plus the cream. Turn the heat up and rotate until bubbling and thickened. Serve on the slices of fried French bread.

Boeuf à la mode Caroline

Caroline Spencer, my downstairs neighbour, has come up with an excellent *Boeuf à la Mode* of her own design; a great dish for this time of year, fairly expensive but consider it a treat.

SERVES 8—12

1.5–1.75kg (3–4 lb) beef
225g (8 oz) unsmoked streaky bacon
oil or good beef dripping
4 medium carrots, sliced
12 button onions, peeled
1 celery stick and 1 leek, chopped
a pig's trotter or a calf's foot

1 tablespoon flour
2 tomatoes, skinned and diced
bay leaf
about 12 peppercorns
300ml (½ pint) white wine
450ml (¾ pint) good beef stock
salt

Preheat the oven to 150°C/300°F/Gas 2.

Get the best beef you can afford. It should be well marbled with fat; really good rump or sirloin is ideal, but silverside would be fine. Make a few light incisions all over the meat, then wrap it round with the streaky bacon, leaving about half the meat exposed. Secure with string.

In a good heavy casserole, brown the meat rapidly in hot oil or dripping, turning over and over until all sides are sealed. Add the carrots, button onions, celery and leek and the pig's trotter or calf's foot. Lower the heat, then sprinkle the flour over the contents of the pot. Cook gently, stirring the while, until the flour is absorbed. Add the diced tomatoes, bay leaf and peppercorns. Cook for a few minutes, stirring again, then add the wine and stock. Bring to simmering point, then taste for seasoning with a little salt (bearing in mind the saltiness of the bacon). Cover and cook gently on the top of the stove or in the oven for 2½ to 3 hours, until the meat is tender right through when pierced with a skewer.

Remove the meat onto a warm platter, untie the string and discard the bacon. If you think there is too much liquid in the pot, boil briskly until it is reduced to your liking, and adjust the seasoning. Then pour over the meat, slice the meat thickly and serve with egg noodles, or potatoes if you prefer, and a crisp salad of endive and leaves.

Baked egg and spinach pie with pancetta

From Australia, we get this most delicious pie which should or could be made the day before to enable the carving of it.

SERVES 6

butter
1 medium onion
325g (13 oz) blanched spinach
12 eggs
325g (13 oz) cottage cheese
200g (8 oz) sour cream

100g (4 oz) grated cheddar cheese
2 teaspoons sea salt
2 teaspoons freshly ground black pepper
1 tablespoon oil
16 slices pancetta or streaky bacon

Preheat the oven to 180°C/350°F/Gas 4.

Butter and then line with baking-paper a 20–25cm (8–10 inch) round cake tin.

Peel and finely dice the onion. Squeeze the spinach dry and chop it roughly. Break the eggs into a large bowl and mix together just enough to break them up, but don't beat. Add the cottage cheese, sour cream, grated cheese, salt and pepper; then add the spinach and onion. Combine thoroughly. Pour the mixture into the prepared tin and place in the middle of the oven. Bake for 30–40 minutes until the pie is fairly firm when you shake the tin. Remove from the oven and let it cool. When cold, cover with cling-film and refrigerate overnight or until well chilled as it is impossible to slice when warm.

Preheat the oven to 150°C/300°F/Gas 2.

Remove from the refrigerator and carefully turn the pie out. Slice it into wedges. Place the pie wedges on a non-stick baking-tray and cover them with foil. Place them in the oven to warm through for about 10 minutes. Heat the oil in a frying pan and cook the pancetta or bacon until it is crisp. Drain on kitchen paper. To serve, place the warmed pie on warmed plates and top with the pancetta. This is very good eaten with the *Roast Tomatoes* on page 110.

Autumn braised leg of lamb

'I shall entice them to eat me speedily.' The writer of these words was St Ignatius of Antioch who had been condemned to death for his faith and was about to be thrown into the arena with the wild beasts. 'I pray they will be prompt with me,' he continued – let's hope they were. It is his feast day on 17 October; on the 18th, St Luke's, patron saint of artists; and the 19th is the day of St John de Brebeuf and Companions who were the first Jesuit missionaries to Canada and North America. Their area was from Nova Scotia to Maryland, but they were captured and vilely tortured to death by the Red Indians who didn't care for their interference – this was in 1642–49. Their deaths occurred in Auriesville, New York. What a tale. Let us therefore go to the antipodes for some refreshment. Here is a nice way of cooking the relatively cheap New Zealand lamb which has a very good flavour – but do thaw it out completely.

SERVES 6

1 teaspoon dry English mustard
1 teaspoon ground ginger
1 tablespoon plain flour
salt and freshly ground black pepper
1.5kg (3½ lb) leg New Zealand lamb

2 leeks, sliced
2 carrots, sliced
4 medium potatoes, quartered
300ml (½ pint) cider
2 sprigs fresh rosemary

Preheat the oven to 190°C/375°F/Gas 5.

Mix together the mustard, ginger, flour and salt and pepper to taste. Rub all over the lamb, pressing it in. Put all the vegetables into a large covered casserole or roasting-tin big enough to take the lamb. Pour in the cider and add the sprigs of rosemary. Place the leg of lamb on top of the vegetables, cover with a tight-fitting lid or foil and roast for one hour.

Uncover and return to the oven at the same temperature until tender and depending on how pink you like it. Another quarter of an hour for really pink, half an hour for just pink, and a whole hour for thoroughly cooked through, which I do not recommend. Place on a nice warm charger with the vegetables and juices around it.

Alaskan hotpot

You are all probably stuffed to the gills by now, so I thought we would have a simple little dish to be hashed up. This is no *haute cuisine* but a surprisingly comforting supper dish – the sort of mess to please the children, I hope.

SERVES 4

550g (1¼ lb) fairly waxy potatoes

3 x 425g (15 oz) tins red Alaska salmon

40g (1½ oz) butter

40g (1½ oz) plain flour

450ml (15 fluid oz) milk

350g (12 oz) leeks, trimmed and sliced

175g (6 oz) sweetcorn kernels

175g (6 oz) frozen peas

175g (6 oz) button mushrooms, sliced

salt

freshly ground pepper

Tabasco (optional)

olive oil

fennel seeds (optional)

Cook the potatoes in boiling water until they are beginning to soften but are still firm. Drain and peel.

Drain and reserve the juice from the tinned salmon. Break the fish into large flakes, discarding any skin or bones. Melt the butter in a large ovenproof casserole, stir in the flour and cook for a minute. Remove from the heat and gradually stir in 250ml (8 fluid oz) of the fish juice, followed by the milk. Return to the heat and slowly bring to the boil, stirring the while. Simmer for 3–5 minutes until the sauce has thickened.

Stir all the vegetables into the sauce and cook for 3 minutes before gently and carefully folding in the salmon flakes. Season to taste with sea salt and freshly ground pepper, maybe a drop or so of Tabasco. Slice the potatoes and arrange daintily, overlapping on the top of the casserole.

Brush all over with olive oil and scatter with fennel seeds if you fancy. Cover and bake in a preheated oven at 190°C/375°F/Gas 5, for about an hour until the potatoes are tender. Remove the lid for the last 20 minutes of cooking so that the potatoes get nice and brown.

Southern Italian fried chicken

It is always a treat to go to Nancy and Michael Lambton's house for Sunday lunch. Michael is one of those natural cooks who, as far as I am concerned, always produces the most delicious food, whatever it may be. His last offering was the best fried chicken I have ever had – which I have adapted slightly for your delectation.

SERVES 4

1.5–1.75kg (3–4 lb) chicken

2 chillies, crushed and chopped

4 tablespoons olive oil

4 tablespoons Italian dry vermouth

2 tablespoons lemon juice

2 plump garlic cloves, crushed

1 small onion, finely sliced

1 dessertspoon dry English mustard

sprig of rosemary

sprig of thyme

sprig of sage

bay leaf

flour, seasoned

breadcrumbs

sesame seeds

paprika

salt and pepper

2 eggs, beaten

sunflower oil

For the tomato sauce:

1 medium onion, finely chopped

2 garlic cloves, crushed and chopped

4 tablespoons olive oil

25g (1 oz) butter

the liquid from the marinade

1 x 400g (14 oz) tin chopped Italian tomatoes

1 teaspoon caster sugar

salt and black pepper

6 fresh basil leaves

Joint the chicken into eight bits, or buy pieces if you prefer. Make a marinade from the crushed and chopped chillies (take great care to wash your hands thoroughly after this operation or you may touch your eyes inadvertently, with dire results), olive oil, vermouth, lemon juice, garlic, onion, mustard and herbs. Mix well together, stir in the chicken pieces, and marinate for six hours, turning them frequently.

When ready, remove the pieces from the marinade and squeeze

any liquid and bits and pieces from them. Pat dry with paper towels. Strain the marinade and reserve the liquid.

Make the tomato sauce now. Gently sauté the onion and garlic in the oil and butter until soft and yellow, add the tomatoes, the marinade liquid, caster sugar, and salt and black pepper to taste. Cover and simmer for 15 minutes. Mix in the torn-up basil leaves and cook for a further five minutes. Use sieved or not, as you desire.

Back to the chicken: have a plastic bag with about two tablespoons of seasoned flour in it, a bowl with breadcrumbs seasoned to taste with the sesame seeds and paprika, and another bowl with the two well-beaten eggs at the ready. Flour the pieces of chicken by shaking them in the bag, coat with the beaten egg, then roll in the breadcrumb mixture. Fry gently in heated shallow oil (I used sunflower) until crisp and golden and cooked through, about 10 to 15 minutes on each side. Keep warm in a low oven if you have to do batches, laying on some paper towels to drain excess oil. Serve with the tomato sauce.

Autumn Accompaniments

Celeriac purée

**I think celeriac purée is an ideal dish to go with most game
and particularly good with pheasant.**

SERVES 4

1 celeriac (about 350g/ 12 oz)
250g (9 oz) potatoes
50g (2 oz) unsalted butter

300ml (10 fluid oz) crème fraîche
salt and pepper

Peel the celeriac and potatoes and cut into quarters. Cook the celeriac in boiling salted water for 20 minutes, then add the potatoes and boil for a further 20 minutes. Drain through a sieve. Purée the lot through a moulinette or a blender. Mix in the butter and the crème fraîche. Beat well with a whisk until the purée is light and smooth. Season to taste and reheat before serving. A *bain-marie* is probably the best way.

Roast tomatoes

**These succulent tomatoes are very good eaten with
the *Baked Egg and Spinach Pie*, on page 103.**

SERVES 6

1 2 ripe tomatoes
1 5 0ml (5 fluid oz) best olive oil

40ml (1 ½ fluid oz) balsamic vinegar
freshly ground black pepper

Preheat the oven to 150°C/300°F/Gas 2.
Halve the tomatoes horizontally and place
them on a baking-tray. Roast for one hour.
Mix the oil and vinegar together. Take the
tomatoes out of the oven and
sprinkle with the oil and
vinegar mixture. Grind the
pepper over them, then return
to the oven for another hour
or until the tomatoes are soft
and caramelised around the edges.
These tomatoes will keep for at least a
week in the refrigerator. Store them
covered with olive oil in a sealed
container. A good thing to have up
your sleeve at any time. Try to get
the best-flavoured tomatoes you
can buy. Another good thing to have
with the pie would be some
splendid mushrooms.

Garlic mushrooms

This is what I call boy-scout cooking but none the less good for that.
Autumn is the mushroom-hunting season and, if you are clever enough, you
can find them in the woods or fields. If not, try to buy something a little better than
the ubiquitous white button. This also makes a tasty little first course.

SERVES 4

4 tablespoons olive oil
50g (2 oz) butter
450g (1 lb) mushrooms, wiped and
quartered
2 cloves garlic, crushed

Maldon salt and freshly ground
black pepper
about 2 tablespoons chopped parsley
wedges of lemon
16 cloves garlic, peeled and whole

Heat the oil and butter in a large frying pan, add the mushrooms and
sauté over a medium heat for three minutes. Stir in the crushed garlic
and sprinkle with Maldon salt and sauté for another one or two minutes. Add several turns of the peppermill and the chopped parsley.
Taste the seasoning, transfer to a warm dish and serve with wedges of
lemon and the whole cloves of garlic which you have fried gently until
soft and golden. They will be sweet and succulent.

Céleri rémoulade

A good thing to have up your sleeve to go with baked meats is a salad of celeriac mayonnaise. This one is from that excellent food writer Marie-Pierre Moine.

S E R V E S 4

For the mayonnaise

1 egg yolk

120ml (4 fluid oz) olive oil

1 tablespoon Dijon mustard

1 teaspoon white wine vinegar

2 small gherkins, chopped

sea salt

freshly ground black pepper

1 tablespoon finely chopped parsley

For the celeriac

2 tablespoons lemon juice

450g (1 lb) celeriac root, peeled and grated

Whisk the egg yolk in a china bowl, then gradually whisk in the olive oil until you have a thick, smooth mayonnaise. Flavour with the mustard, vinegar, chopped gherkins, salt, pepper and parsley.

Now bring some lightly salted water to the boil in a saucepan, add the lemon juice and tip in the grated celeriac. Blanch for 1–2 minutes. Drain well and squeeze out any excess moisture with your hands, then spread the celeriac on a tea-cloth and pat dry.

Adjust the seasoning of the mayonnaise which should be quite piquant and peppery; stir in the celeriac until coated all over with the mayonnaise. Chill for at least 15 minutes, or longer if more convenient. Just before serving, stir again and sprinkle some more parsley on top.

Autumn Desserts

Pumpkin cheesecake

I don't like pumpkin puddings but you may. Try this one.

SERVES 6—8

750g (1½ lb) slice of pumpkin
450g (1 lb) Philadelphia cream cheese
175g (6 oz) caster sugar
1 teaspoon grated nutmeg

¼ teaspoon ground ginger
salt
2 eggs, beaten

For the base:

50g (2 oz) softened butter
65g (2½ oz) sugar

1 egg
150g (5 oz) plain flour

Preheat the oven to 190°C/375°F/Gas 5.

Begin by making a pumpkin purée: wrap a large slice of pumpkin in foil and bake in the oven for one hour. Scrape away the seeds and pith, then peel it. Purée through a sieve or processor. Weigh out 450g (1 lb) for use.

Turn up the oven to 200°C/400°F/Gas 6. For the base, cream together the butter and sugar, beat in the egg, add the flour and mix well. Roll out the dough on a piece of floured grease-proof paper and use it to line the bottom and 5cm (2 inches) up the sides of a 23cm (9 inch) spring-form tin. Bake in the preheated oven for five minutes.

For the filling, combine the Philadelphia cream cheese at room temperature with the caster sugar until well blended. Mix in the 450g

(1 lb) of pumpkin, grated nutmeg, ground ginger and a good pinch of salt. Add the eggs, one at a time, blending well after each addition. Pour the filling into the tin. Bake in the oven at 180°C/350°F/Gas 4, for 50 minutes.

Allow to cool for an hour before removing from the oven. Loosen the rim of the tin, cool, then chill the cheesecake but do not remove the rim until just before serving. Decorate with whipped cream and marzipan fruits, if you like.

Charlotte clementines

This receipt comes courtesy of the beautiful Simon Snow.

SERVES 6

8 slices good white bread
50g (2 oz) butter

12 clementines
75g (3 oz) sugar

Preheat the oven to 180°C/350°F/Gas 4.

Fry the bread in the butter on both sides. Cut off the crusts and roll out thinly while still warm. Cut into fingers, leaving a circle for the bottom and top of six small ramekin dishes; the fingers of fried bread should overlap each other round the sides of the ramekins. Peel the clementines, separate the segments and caramelise them in the sugar for 1½ minutes. Add a little butter, pack the mixture tightly into the ramekins and seal with a round of fried bread. Cover each dish tightly with foil and steam for half an hour in a tray of water in a medium oven – the water should reach halfway up the sides of the dishes.

Turn out each one and grill to crisp them. Serve with crème anglaise or just cream.

Sudden death

My friend Ian Scott called one day asking for the receipt of the killer chocolate pudding from Patricius Senhouse, my old china from Cumberland. Here it is.

SERVES 4

225g (8 oz) digestive biscuits
225g (8 oz) Menier chocolate or the like
225g (8 oz) unsalted butter
50g (2 oz) caster sugar

2 eggs
50g (2 oz) chopped walnuts
50g (2 oz) chopped glacé cherries
85ml (3 fluid oz) rum, brandy or whisky

Grease and line a 450g (1 lb) tin or container. No cooking is required, so it can be anything that takes your fancy. Crush the biscuits roughly in a plastic bag. Melt the chocolate in a bowl set over hot water. Cream the butter and sugar, then gradually beat in the eggs until thick and frothy. Fold in the chocolate, biscuits, nuts, cherries and liquor. Pour into the tin and chill overnight. (It can also be frozen.) Turn out and decorate with more cherries and walnuts. Serve with whipped cream. Force yourself.

Floreat Etona

Eton College was founded on 12 September 1440 so I thought I would dedicate this forgotten autumn pudding to the former headmaster, Eric Anderson, my friend and fan.

SERVES 4

300ml (10 fluid oz) breadcrumbs

75g (3 oz) finely chopped suet

50g (2 oz) sugar

50g (2 oz) currants

50g (2 oz) sultanas

or 25g (1 oz) shredded candied peel

a pinch of nutmeg

a pinch of salt

2 eggs

1 tablespoon brandy

a knob of butter

cooking oil

Mix the breadcrumbs, suet, sugar, currants, sultanas or peel, nutmeg and salt together. Beat the eggs with the brandy until frothy, then pour into the dry ingredients and mix thoroughly.

Cover the basin and let the mixture stand for at least an hour. Form the mixture into round or cork-shaped pieces. Fry very gently in butter with a touch of tasteless cooking oil, turning them frequently. Or, if you prefer, put the mixture into 4 well-buttered dariole moulds and bake in a preheated oven for 25 minutes at 190°C/375°F/Gas 5.

Serve as hot as possible with a good wine or brandy sauce.

Patrick's bread and butter pudding

My friend and fellow cook Patrick Williams is also a fine flautist, but in 1987 he was involved in a collision with a juggernaut whilst riding his bicycle and lost all his front teeth, not good for flautists. However, after five years of painful dental surgery the teeth are back and he can play the flute once more. He has his own strong views about cooking which he does superbly, and this is his family's method of making proper bread and butter pudding. I shall relate it to you as told to me. The essential ingredients are stale baguettes and Irish whiskey.

---

unsalted butter, softened	3 eggs
stale baguettes	600ml (1 pint) milk
raisins or currants	Irish whiskey
sugar	

Butter a soufflé dish lavishly with softened unsalted butter. Cut the stale baguettes into rather thin slices, crusts and all, some to line the dish, the others to make up the bulk. Butter each slice, again lavishly. Press the buttered side to the wall of the dish, then fill up the well with the rest of the slices buttered side down, sprinkling raisins or currants in between the layers; the last layer should be butter-side up and sprinkled with sugar.

For the 'custard', the ratio is three whole eggs to one pint of milk. Blend the eggs and milk (half cream if you prefer), add a little sugar to taste and a very generous slug of Irish whiskey. Pour all this over the bread. Place in another bowl to catch overflow, then press down. Cover with a bit of foil and place weights on top. Leave for at least six hours overnight. Pour the overflow back into the pudding and place in a preheated oven at 230°C/450°F/Gas 8, for 30–40 minutes, after which it will rise above itself like a lovely soufflé.

Winter

starters

Black bean soup
Garlic-stuffed mussels
Oyster po-boy
Irish oysters, Chinese style

Potato and leek rosti with dolcelatte and
Parma ham
Ruby red risotto
Goat's cheese soufflé

main courses

Smothered chicken breasts
Lapin aux pruneaux
Brazilian chopped beef in baked pumpkin
Steak and kidney pudding

Tourte des Terre-Nuevas
Aberdeen Angus beef casserole
Poulet béarnais
Turkey thighs with pancetta

accompaniments

Rosti
Broad bean purée
Prem's peas

A receipt of the señor which cooked
itself at the goodness of God
Prune sauce

desserts

Whisky galore
Bananas as I arrange them for guests of
the last minute

Yogurt, cheese and honey mould
Suffolk frozen lemon pudding

Winter Starters

Black bean soup

On 4 February candles are crossed at the throat for St Blaise.
Sore throats and colds abound during winter and my thoughts turn to
wonderful soups made properly; comforting and nutritious for the aching throat
or diminished appetite. This serves as a very filling first course but also makes a
perfect lunch or supper dish on its own with some good bread. It comes from
America via the Caribbean, and especially Cuba, and is wonderfully dramatic
to look upon, jet-black with sliced lemon and eggs staring at you.

SERVES 6–8

450g (1 lb) dried black beans
2 litres (3½ pints) water for the soaking
40g (1½ oz) butter
2 big onions, chopped
2 fat cloves garlic, chopped and crushed
3 celery sticks, chopped
bouquet garni of parsley, thyme and
bay leaf
1–1.5kg (2–3 lb) veal bones
1 ham bone, if you can get one

1.5 litres (2½ pints) proper chicken stock
6 peppercorns
1 litre (1¾ pints) water
2 tablespoons lemon juice
1 teaspoon salt
150ml (¼ pint) brandy, or Madeira or
medium sherry
1 lemon, very thinly sliced
2 hard-boiled eggs, chopped
chopped parsley

Soak the beans in the water overnight. Strain and discard the water.
Melt the butter in a large saucepan and cook the onions, garlic
and celery gently until soft but not browned. Add the bouquet garni,

veal bones, ham bone, chicken stock, peppercorns, beans and water.

Bring to the boil for 10 minutes, then reduce to a simmer; skim the top, leave partially covered and cook for four hours until the beans mash easily when pressed. Remove the bones and the bouquet garni. Purée the soup through a food-mill; add the lemon juice, salt and the brandy, Madeira or sherry. If the soup seems too thick, dilute with some more hot stock. Taste for seasoning and serve piping hot in warmed soup-plates. Garnish with the lemon slices, chopped hard-boiled eggs and chopped parsley. Delectable.

Garlic-stuffed mussels

If oysters are not your thing, try mussels which are in fine fettle during this season.

SERVES 4

1.75kg (4 lb) fresh mussels
175g (6 oz) butter
4–6 cloves garlic, crushed

chopped parsley
juice of 1 lemon
50g (2 oz) fine white breadcrumbs

Wash and debeard the mussels thoroughly. Discard any that are broken or open. Place in a shallow, heavy saucepan. Cover with a tight-fitting lid and cook over a high heat for 5–7 minutes, shaking occasionally. Remove the top shell from each mussel and arrange the bottom shell with the flesh in a dish. Melt the butter, add garlic, parsley and lemon juice. Pour over the mussels, sprinkle with the breadcrumbs, then grill or bake until golden brown. Splendid.

Oyster po-boy

**There is a famous Louisiana sandwich which can be stuffed
with any number of fillings, but here the oysters are simply grilled with
a herb-and-garlic dressing.**

SERVES 4

16 gigas oysters
3 tablespoons olive oil
25g (1 oz) unsalted butter
1 garlic clove, peeled and crushed
1 tablespoon freshly chopped parsley
freshly ground black pepper

1 teaspoon lemon juice
4 rashers streaky bacon,
rinds removed
2 baguettes – the small variety
extra olive oil
Tabasco

Grill the oysters, flat shell uppermost, until the shells open slightly.
The oyster juices will start to bubble out of the shells after three to
five minutes. Hold the oysters in a cloth, insert a knife between the
shells, twist off the top shell and discard. Slip the knife under the flesh
to free it. Remove the oysters with their juices and place in a bowl.

Heat the olive oil and butter together with the garlic. Add
parsley, pepper and lemon juice; no need for salt. Stretch the bacon
with the blade of a knife, cut into four and make small rolls. Thread
the oysters and bacon onto four slightly oiled skewers. Brush the
oysters with the sauce and grill for two minutes each side, basting
frequently.

Halve the baguettes lengthways, toast cut sides until golden,
then dribble with olive oil. Remove oysters and bacon from the
skewers and arrange on the bread. Spoon over a little more sauce and
hand round the Tabasco, to be added to taste.

Irish oysters, Chinese style

As oysters are meant to be the food of love, I thought you might like some of the ways to deal with the gigas or Pacific oyster other than swallowing it raw, to celebrate St Valentine. They are much cheaper than native oysters and not as good in my opinion. I wouldn't dream of cooking a native, but I think it improves the gigas, especially when they are sold in the spawning season and get very fat and creamy in texture. They are sold all year round for some reason, which I think is a mistake, but doubtless it brings in the shekels.

········ S E R V E S 2 ········

1 small carrot, peeled and shredded
1 thin slice fresh ginger root, peeled and shredded
3 tablespoons light soy sauce
1 tablespoon sherry
½–1 teaspoon Tabasco

2 teaspoons sesame oil
3 spring onions, trimmed and shredded
12 gigas oysters
a few leaves fresh coriander or parsley
½ a small, fresh red chilli, de-seeded and finely chopped (optional)

Blanch the carrot in boiling water for one minute, add the ginger for the last few seconds. Drain well. Mix the soy sauce, sherry, Tabasco and sesame oil, then add the carrot, ginger and the spring onions. Scrub the oysters, place in a saucepan with a little boiling water, cover, bring back to the boil and simmer until the shells open, about five minutes. Remove from the heat. Insert a short-bladed knife between the shells and twist off the top shell. Slip the knife under the oyster to free the flesh from the shell. Arrange the oysters in their shells and spoon a little of the sauce over each one. Garnish with fresh coriander or parsley, and sprinkle over a little chopped red chilli if you wish. A dainty dish for a loving couple.

Potato and leek rosti with dolcelatte and Parma ham

Now for a mixture of Switzerland and Italy.

.... S E R V E S 4 ....

150g (5 oz) trimmed leeks
450g (1 lb) waxy potatoes
25g (1 oz) plain flour
1 egg, beaten
salt and pepper

oil for frying
100g (4 oz) dolcelatte cheese, cut
into 8 slices
8 slices Parma ham

Cut the leeks lengthways, then slice thinly and place in a bowl large enough to receive the potatoes. Either grate the potatoes coarsely or shred in a food processor. Add to the leeks, sprinkle on the flour and toss together. Stir in the egg, season and mix well. Divide the mixture into eight heaps. Heat enough oil in a large frying pan to shallow fry, then drop four heaps of the mixture into the pan. Cook over moderate to high heat until golden brown, turn over and cook the other side. Lift out and drain on kitchen paper, then keep warm in the oven while cooking the rest of the rosti. Before serving, place a slice of cheese and a slice of ham in folds on top of each rosti. Serve at once.

Ruby red risotto

If you're after a receipt for St Valentine's day, try this startling red risotto which I was served by Willie Landels. It is highly original, I should think, amazing to behold and most delicious, though it would make my lovely colleague, Clare Asquith, tremble with horror as she shies from beetroot as I do from spiders.

SERVES 4

225g (8 oz) arborio rice
3 medium-size cooked beetroots
250ml (8 fluid oz) milk
900ml (1 ½ pints) chicken or veal stock
2 tablespoons olive oil

25g (1 oz) butter
1 medium-size onion
150ml (5 fluid oz) red or white wine
salt and freshly ground pepper
fresh Parmesan cheese

Risotto is not a pilaf or anything to do with the dishes requiring that every grain of rice should be separate; it is therefore essential to use the arborio rice which has plump, succulent and absorbent grains. Buy the white grains, never the yellowish ones.

Put the beetroots and the milk in a blender, and whizz until smooth. Have the stock heating in a pouring saucepan. In another saucepan put the olive oil and butter to melt. Peel and chop the onion very finely, add to the oil and cook gently until golden but not brown. Stir in the rice until it is well impregnated with the oil and butter, pour in the wine and let it continue to cook gently until absorbed. Now add 600ml (1 pint) of the stock, cup by cup. Let it cook and absorb, but keep your eye on it, giving the odd stir; pour in the beetroot mixture and season with salt and freshly ground pepper. At the end of the cooking, which will be about 20 minutes, stir continuously to prevent sticking to the bottom of the pan and add the last of the stock if necessary.

The rice should be a creamy consistency like a bowl of porridge but still have a slight bite to it. Add a tablespoon of freshly grated Parmesan cheese, turn off the heat and let it rest for a couple of minutes, when it will be *ben mantecato* as the Italians put it. Serve at once with more Parmesan on the side.

Goat's cheese soufflé

Towards the end of December we enter the Capricorn sign. Not that I set any store by these much-vaunted occurrences, but I thought it might be jolly to produce a goat's cheese soufflé. I believe it originated at some splendid restaurant in San Francisco. Very rich and quite marvellous. This receipt will do for eight people as a first course.

.... SERVES 8 ....

75g (3 oz) unsalted butter
5 level tablespoons plain flour
350ml (12 fluid oz) single cream
250ml (8 fluid oz) whipping cream
salt
freshly ground pepper
cayenne
grated nutmeg
5 egg yolks, beaten
175g (6 oz) strong goat's cheese,
crumbled

6 egg whites
2 level teaspoons dried thyme

Melt the butter in a saucepan, stir in the
flour and cook gently for a few minutes;
let it cool a little. Mix the two creams
and bring to the boil in another saucepan,
then whisk into the prepared roux. Season to taste
with the salt, freshly ground pepper, cayenne and
grated nutmeg. Place the saucepan over barely
simmering water (use a *bain-marie* if you have one),
cover and leave the sauce to cook for an hour, giving
it the odd stir now and then.

Preheat the oven to 230°C/450°F/Gas 8.

Remove the pan from the water and cool slightly before
stirring in the beaten egg yolks. Add two-thirds of the cheese
and check the seasoning. Stir thoroughly, put the remaining

cheese on top, and pepper it well. Beat the egg whites until very stiff, then fold into the cheese sauce.

Have ready a lavishly buttered shallow, oval gratin dish (not your usual soufflé dish), about 30cm (12 inches) long. Pour the soufflé mixture into the dish more or less evenly, and sprinkle the top with the dried thyme. Place in the top part of the oven, about 12 minutes in a metal dish, a bit longer for an earthenware one. It should appear brown and puffy on the top and sides and soft and creamy within. *Baveuse* is the term, methinks.

Winter Main Courses

Smothered chicken breasts

Here is a good dish for January – when we all start trying to get back to normal, having finished with the Epiphany and dismantled all the cards and tinsel. Saint Hilary's day is on 13 January. He was the first person to write Latin hymns but only three remain. One about the Trinity is 70 verses long – imagine.

The following receipt comes from a booklet published to celebrate Llanedwen Church on the Plas Newydd estate of Marquess and Lady Anglesey. It is the only church in Wales in regular use to be lit entirely by candles. Standing just above the Menai strait, its spire is a well-known landmark for sailors.

Lady Anglesey says this dish meets her two main culinary requirements: 'It must have a strong flavour to suit my husband's taste buds and it must be reheatable to suit my convenience.'

SERVES 4

1 tablespoon green peppercorns in brine
2 cloves garlic, peeled
100g (4 oz) cottage cheese
1 teaspoon dried mixed herbs

75g (3 oz) butter
salt and a pinch of paprika
4 boned chicken breasts

Drain the peppercorns. Chop the garlic finely. In a bowl combine the cottage cheese, garlic, peppercorns, herbs, butter and seasonings. Mix to a smooth paste. Spread the boned chicken breasts with the paste and place in a medium-sized iron casserole. Cook in a hot oven, 200°C/400°F/Gas 6, for 30 minutes, basting frequently.

131

Remove from oven to eat or to be reheated when needed. I think I would just leave them coated in the paste ready to cook rather than reheating, as I find chicken breasts can go stringy if cooked twice.

Lapin aux pruneaux

I was once on one of those quizzes and was told to make a dish from rabbit, prunes and mustard, a curious trio. I did my best but what I was really thinking of was a lovely dish as follows:

SERVES 6

1 rabbit or about 6 pieces of rabbit

175g (6 oz) of prunes

1 tablespoon olive oil

15g (½ oz) butter

15g (½ oz) plain flour

200ml (7 fluid oz) red wine

300ml (½ pint) chicken or
game stock

2 garlic cloves, crushed

bouquet garni of thyme, bay leaf
and parsley

salt and pepper

1 tablespoon chopped parsley

100g (4 oz) bacon lardons, sautéed
(optional)

50g (2oz) raisins (optional)

For the marinade:

150ml (¼ pint) red wine

1 large bouquet garni

1 onion, coarsely chopped

1 carrot, coarsely chopped

6 black peppercorns, slightly crushed

1 tablespoon olive oil

Cut the rabbit into six pieces if whole, and place in a glass or china bowl. Mix in the marinade ingredients and pour the oil on top. Cover and leave at room temperature for four to 12 hours, giving it the odd turn.

Pour boiling water over the prunes, cover and leave to soak for three hours or so.

Remove the rabbit from the marinade with a slotted spoon and pat dry with paper towels. Heat the oil and butter in a frying pan or shallow casserole and brown the rabbit pieces all over. Remove from the pan, add the carrot and onion from the marinade and fry gently until soft. Sprinkle the flour over the vegetables and cook, stirring until the flour browns. Stir in the marinade and the wine and bring to the boil. Add the stock, garlic, and bouquet garni and season with salt and pepper. Replace the rabbit pieces, cover and simmer for 25 minutes. Transfer them to another shallow casserole and strain the sauce over them through a mouli or a sieve, pressing the vegetables through. Drain the prunes, add to the rabbit. Cover and simmer for 10–15 minutes or until the rabbit and prunes are tender.

Transfer the rabbit to a serving dish and spoon the prunes over the top. If necessary, reduce the sauce by boiling until it just coats the back of a spoon. Adjust seasoning and spoon over the rabbit. Sprinkle with parsley before serving. You can add the sautéed bacon lardons and the raisins to the rabbit for the last 15 minutes of cooking if you wish.

Brazilian chopped beef in baked pumpkin

This wonderful receipt for *Picadinho com abóbora* comes from the Brazilian embassy. Although it is meant to be done with beef, I'm sure it would do marvels for left-over Christmas turkey and would be a very festive-looking supper dish for Boxing Day. Accompany with plain, boiled white rice, some preserved chilli peppers or hot pepper sauce and a simple but beautiful green salad with a good dressing.

S E R V E S 8 — 1 0

1 x 2kg (4lb) pumpkin
salt and freshly ground pepper
a few gratings of mace
250ml (8 fluid oz) good chicken stock
25ml (1 fluid oz) cachaça
or dry white rum
1kg (2lb) beef sirloin or topside,
trimmed of all fat
2 tablespoons red wine vinegar
a good pinch of cinnamon and
ground cloves
175ml (6 fluid oz) olive oil
1 sweet yellow pepper and 1 sweet red
pepper, cored, de-seeded and diced

2 medium onions, chopped
2 cloves of garlic, chopped
2 tablespoons tomato paste
2 large tomatoes, peeled, de-seeded
and chopped
250ml (8 fluid oz) beef stock
1 small hot chilli, de-seeded and
diced
1 tablespoon Worcestershire sauce
3 tablespoons chopped parsley
10 green olives, stoned and chopped
2 tablespoons large capers, washed,
drained and dried

Preheat the oven to 190°C/375°F/Gas 5. Cut a circle about 7.5cm (3 inches) from the stem of the pumpkin to form a lid. Scoop out the seeds from the pumpkin and clean away the fibres. Lightly salt and pepper the inside and add a pinch or two of mace. Add the chicken stock and cachaça or rum. Replace the lid to fit, rub the outside of the pumpkin with vegetable oil, and place on a well-oiled baking pan. Bake for 50 minutes, or until the interior flesh is tender and the exterior is still firm.

Remove from the oven and allow to cool for 5 minutes. Slide a large spatula under the pumpkin and carefully transfer to a warm serving platter. Remove the lid, and extract the liquid from the pumpkin with a bulb baster. Replace the lid, cover the pumpkin with foil and keep warm until ready to fill with the chopped beef.

Meanwhile, as the pumpkin has been cooking, slice the meat into 2.5mm (¼-inch) slices. Put the slices in a flat pan, cover with cling-film and place in the freezer for 30 minutes. Then cut the slices into small dice, place in a large bowl and toss with the vinegar, cinnamon and cloves. Marinate for 20 minutes. In a large frying pan heat 50ml (2 fluid oz) of the olive oil over a medium heat; when it begins to smoke, add the diced meat and brown quickly, stirring the while. Remove the meat from the heat and strain off the juice into a bowl. Reserve the juice and the meat separately.

Heat another 50ml (2 fluid oz) of the olive oil and sauté the yellow and red peppers until they are limp (about 5 minutes). Remove with a slotted spoon and add to the meat mixture. Add the remaining olive oil to the pan and sauté the onions and garlic until golden brown. Add the tomato paste and stir occasionally for about 5 minutes until the mixture darkens and thickens. Add the tomatoes, the reserved meat juice and the beef stock. Bring to the boil, reduce the heat and simmer for 10 minutes. Add the onion mixture to the meat mixture, along with the chilli pepper and season with salt and pepper. Return the picadinho to the frying pan and cook over a medium heat at a slow simmer for 20 to 30 minutes until all the ingredients are tender and most of the liquid is absorbed. Add the Worcestershire sauce (or Brazilian Jimmy sauce, if you have it), parsley, olives and capers and cook for another 5 minutes.

Using a thin-bladed paring knife, remove the pumpkin lid and extract any remaining liquid from the well of the pumpkin with the bulb baster. Fill the pumpkin with the picadinho and set the lid on top. Serve by scooping out a little of the pumpkin flesh with some of the picadinho.

Steak and kidney pudding

I once received a letter at the *Spectator* from Nigel Sturgeon of Tunbridge Wells requesting a receipt for good old steak and kidney pudding for his surgeon friend in Alaska. Maybe they don't have suet in Alaska. Anyhow, here it is.

SERVES 6

For the filling:

900g (2 lb) rump steak	300ml (½ pint) red wine
1 whole ox kidney	300ml (½ pint) beef stock
2 tablespoons seasoned flour	bouquet garni of bay leaf, parsley and
1 large onion, chopped	thyme
75g (3 oz) butter	

For the suet crust:

275g (10 oz) self-raising flour	¾ teaspoon dried thyme
1 level teaspoon baking powder	100g (4 oz) chopped or grated suet
½ teaspoon salt	cold water
freshly ground pepper	

Preheat the oven to 150°C/300°F/Gas 2.

Cut the steak into strips, 5cm (2 inches) by 2.5cm (1 inch), and slice the kidney, removing all fat and skin from both, and shake in the seasoned flour (in a plastic bag). Fry the onion in the butter until browned, then remove with a slotted spoon to a plate. Fry the meats rapidly in batches to brown all over, then transfer to a casserole. Pour the wine and stock into the frying pan and boil for a moment or two, scraping the bottom for scraps. Pour over the meat, add the onions and the bouquet garni, cover with the lid and cook in the preheated oven for 1½ hours until almost cooked. This can all be done in advance.

To make the crust – mix all the dry ingredients in a large bowl, making sure the suet is evenly distributed. Stir in cold water with a knife to make a firm dough, and knead with fingertips until smooth. Roll out on a floured surface into a big enough circle to cover a 1.75

litre (3 pint) pudding basin. Cut out a quarter segment and set aside for the lid.

Butter the pudding basin and place the three-quarter circle of pastry into it, joining the ends so it fits as smoothly as possible, and leave about an inch overhanging the rim. Check the seasoning of the meat filling and scoop into the basin – it should come to an inch below the rim. Roll out the remaining pastry to fit as a lid. Brush the edges with water, lift on a rolling-pin and cover the basin and press the edges together firmly to seal. Cut a square of foil (double thickness) 5cm (2 inches) wider across than the basin top, and make a pleat in the middle. Press the edges under the rim of the basin, pleating as you go, and secure with string or elastic, making a handle to facilitate handling; or cut a long strip of foil (double thickness) to go under the bowl and hang over the sides of the saucepan or steamer.

Put the pudding in the top half of a steamer and when the water is boiling in the lower half place on top, cover and simmer for 1½ to 2 hours, keeping an eye on the water which may need topping up with more boiling water. If you don't have a steamer, boil water in a large saucepan and place the pudding basin on an upside-down saucer; the water should come three-quarters of the way up the basin. Cover with the lid. When the pudding is cooked remove it from the pan and take off the foil cover and strings. Wrap in a white napkin and serve immediately with cabbage or sprouts. Variations can be made with the addition of 225g (8 oz) mushrooms or a dozen or so fresh oysters mixed in just before pouring the meats into the pastry. Old, tough game birds make very good steamed puddings. Over to you, Alaska.

Tourte des Terre-Nuevas

The patron saint of children and sailors, the great St Nicholas, has his feast
day on 6 December and it is interesting that his final transformation into 'Father
Christmas' and 'Santa Claus' occurred among Protestants. Dutch Protestant settlers in
new Amsterdam – now New York – took with them traditions of 'Sinter Claes', which
spread throughout the United States and then back into European children's lore.
Apart from him, we have St Ambrose who baptised St Augustine in 385,
and dear little St Leocadia who was tortured and put to death during the
persecution of the Emperor Diocletian. In this advent to Christmas vein, I thought
it might be a good idea to include a Portuguese fish pie for Christmas Eve,
made of course with salt cod. A purée of turnips or parsnips goes
extremely well with this dish.

SERVES 4

450g (1 lb) dried salt cod
350g (1 lb) good waxy potatoes
1 large onion, chopped
3 shallots, chopped
100g (4 oz) butter

450g (1 lb) puff pastry
2 good tablespoons chopped parsley
salt and freshly ground pepper
300ml (½ pint) thick cream,
slightly heated

Soak the cod for at least 36 hours with changes of water any time you
think of it. Put it in a saucepan with fresh cold water covering it. Bring
slowly to simmering point. As soon as it begins to bubble remove it
from the heat and leave until the skin and bone can be easily removed
from the flakes of fish.

Boil the potatoes in their skins; when ready, drain, peel and cut
into rounds. Fry the chopped onion and shallots in 50g (2 oz) of the
butter until they are soft but not browned.

Preheat the oven to 230°C/450°F/Gas 8.

Cut the pastry in half. Roll one half out and line a 23–25cm
(9–10 inch) tart tin with a removable bottom. Fill with the flaked cod,
the potatoes and the onion mixture. Sprinkle with the parsley, season
with a lot of freshly ground pepper and salt to taste (remember the

cod is still quite salty). Dot with the remaining butter. Roll out the other half of the pastry, brush the outer rim with water and lay it on top of the pie, wet side down, and press the edges together. Cut a circle of 4cm (1 ½ inches) across from the middle of the lid and put it to cook beside the pie on a baking tray. Place the pie in the oven with its little circle and cook for about ½ hour until the pastry is puffed high and golden.

Remove from the tin, if possible onto a fine hot dish or platter, pour the slightly heated cream into the pie through the hole, then cover with its circle of pastry and serve immediately, very hot.

Aberdeen Angus beef casserole

This receipt uses Scottish beef – the best in the world, I reckon.

SERVES 8

1.35kg (3 lb) steak, rump or sirloin
3 tablespoons seasoned flour
2 tablespoons vegetable oil
4 large onions, thinly sliced
4 cloves garlic, crushed
2 tablespoons brown sugar
600ml (1 pint) good beef stock
2 bottles of Leffe Blond Belgian beer
(330ml bottles)

2 tablespoons white wine vinegar
bouquet garni of bay leaf, thyme, celery
and parsley
2 tablespoons French mustard
3 oz softened butter
1 baguette cut into 2.5cm (1 inch) slices
freshly chopped parsley
and thyme

Preheat the oven to 160°C/325°F/Gas 3.

Cut the steak into half-postcard-sized pieces about 1cm (½ inch) thick and toss in the seasoned flour. Heat the vegetable oil in a large casserole, add the beef and sear all over. Add the onions, 2 cloves of garlic, sugar, stock, beer, vinegar and the bouquet garni. Mix together, cover and place in the preheated oven for 2 hours or until tender.

Blend the mustard with the butter and the two remaining garlic cloves and spread one side of each slice of bread. Uncover the casserole and arrange the slices of bread on top, mustard side uppermost. Increase the temperature of the oven to 200°C/400°F/Gas 6. Return casserole to the oven and cook uncovered for a further 15 minutes until the top is crisp and browning. Sprinkle with some fresh chopped parsley and thyme.

Serve with noodles or wild rice, baby carrots and broccoli.

Poulet béarnais

I was given a present by my neighbour Caroline Spencer: a jar of prepared garlic cloves in olive oil, an incredibly useful gift as you can use them for anything you are cooking, from stews and roasts to salads and *crostini*. Put a quantity of whole garlic bulbs on a baking tray in a very low oven, say 110°C/225°F/Gas ¹/₄, and bake for 1–1¹/₂ hours. Let them cool, then peel each clove. Place them in jars and cover with good olive oil. The oil becomes impregnated with the garlic and can be used to give flavour. Just top up the jar with more olive oil.

To continue with this magic bulb, let us indulge in that magnificent dish, chicken cooked on a nest of up to 900g (2 lb) of garlic, if you can face peeling that amount. This may alarm some people but after the cooking the strength of the garlic has evaporated and the cloves taste sweetly delicious. Even if you don't eat them they will impart aroma to the chicken.

SERVES 4–6

from 40 cloves to 900g (2 lb) garlic
1 lemon
1 chicken – 1.75kg (4 lb)
4 sprigs tarragon
salt and freshly ground pepper

25g (1 oz) butter
1 tablespoon olive oil
1 tablespoon Cognac
4 tablespoons dry white vermouth

Preheat the oven to 190°C/375°F/Gas 5.

This is adapted from Frances Bissell who uses 40 garlic cloves.

Peel the cloves (this is facilitated by cutting the root end off first and/or covering in boiling water for ½ minute).

Squeeze the lemon juice over the chicken and rub it well in; put the remains of the lemon into the cavity with the tarragon. Season with salt and freshly ground pepper. Heat the butter and oil in a casserole to fit the chicken, and brown the bird all over. Pour on the Cognac, light it, swivelling the dish until the flames die. Remove the bird, put all the garlic on the bottom of the dish and return the chicken to sit on this garlic nest. Dribble the vermouth over the whole. Cover the casserole and cook in the preheated oven for an hour, remove the lid, baste the breast and cook for a further 15–20 minutes to produce a nice browned skin.

Your kitchen will abound with fragrance and delight. Have some new potatoes and little peas with this feast, or a good tomato salad wouldn't go amiss.

Turkey thighs and pancetta

Most supermarkets have taken to selling skinned turkey thighs lately, nice little hunks of meat which I find have far more flavour than the breast fillets. But you may prefer otherwise, so suit your own fancy. This is what I have done with the thigh pieces.

SERVES 3

6 turkey thighs
sea salt
freshly ground black pepper
2 bay leaves
4 fresh sage leaves or a large pinch of
dried sage

4–5 tablespoons Madeira or
medium sherry
2 tablespoons olive oil
8 juniper berries
12 slices of pancetta
chicken or game stock

Place the turkey thighs in a shallow dish, sprinkle with rock or sea salt and a good grinding of black pepper. Crumble a couple of bay leaves over the meat, and add the sage. Dribble the Madeira or sherry over the top and anoint with the olive oil. Crush the juniper berries and add to the marinade. Leave for about six hours or overnight, turning the turkey over every now and then.

Buy the pancetta at your local Italian delicatessen. This is my answer to that horrible wet bacon we are served with nowadays. It is exactly the same cut of meat as streaky bacon, cured and sometimes smoked. We want the pancetta *stesa*; have it cut into thin slices.

Preheat the oven to 200°C/400°F/Gas 6.

Wrap each turkey piece in two slices of the pancetta, making nice little parcels. Place them in a suitable oven dish, pour the marinade over them and put in a small amount of stock to cover the bottom of the dish. Place in the preheated oven for 30 minutes, turning over at half time.

Even better is to stuff each piece with a very lightly sautéed slice of turkey liver. Serve with glazed carrots, broccoli and purée of potatoes. Darn good.

Winter Accompaniments

Rosti

A very good thing to have with any old cold meat is a sizzling plate of rosti, the quintessential Swiss-German dish. It is also very good for those who have imbibed too much for the breathalyser – I am told it sits like an eiderdown on the fumes. Who knows?

SERVES 6—8

1 kg (2 ¼ lb) firm, waxy potatoes
salt and pepper

50g (2 oz) butter
2 teaspoons oil

Boil the potatoes until just tender. Drain and leave overnight. Next day, peel them, then grate coarsely. Season with salt and pepper. Heat half the butter and oil in a heavy-based, preferably non-stick frying pan, large or small enough to take the potatoes so that they fit in snugly to form a flattish cake. Press the potatoes into the pan and cook over a moderate heat for about 20 minutes, until the bottom is golden brown and crusty. Invert the rosti on to a plate or board. Heat the rest of the butter and oil in the pan, slide the rosti back into the pan, browned side uppermost, and cook the second side. When ready, slide on to a hot plate and serve in wedges. Waxy potatoes are essential or the whole thing goes mushy.

Another version is to cook 100g (4 oz) of diced bacon in the pan before adding the potatoes. Fry the bacon until the fat runs and add a little oil if necessary to just cover the bottom of the pan, then continue as above. When the rosti is ready, sprinkle the top with 150g (5 oz) of grated hard cheese and leave for a minute or two until the cheese is melted. A mixture of Parmesan and gruyère makes a very good topping.

Broad bean purée

This is a painless way of converting late-season or frozen broad beans with their leather jackets into something light and delicious.

SERVES 4

450g (1 lb) prodded broad beans – fresh or frozen
salt
pepper

1 dessertspoonful of chopped summer savory or parsley
50g (2 oz) butter
small tub of crème fraîche

Cook the broad beans without salt until tender. Drain but keep the cooking water. Place the beans in a food processor, season with salt and pepper, add the herbs, butter and crème fraîche and whizz into a purée, adding enough cooking liquor to make it light and slightly sloppy. To achieve perfect smoothness, push the purée through a fine sieve – it depends on how smooth you like it. Pour into a warm dish. This is an excellent accompaniment for roast pork or ham.

Prem's peas

I once had dinner at the house of an Indian couple, Indar and Aruna Pasricha.
It was the first time I had eaten Indian food privately, and what a difference it was.
No violent curry tastes but everything delicately flavoured with suitable spices
and herbs. The peas were a side-dish and the whole dinner was cooked by
their faithful friend and helper, Prem Chand.

SERVES 8

3 tablespoons corn oil
1 large onion, finely chopped
1 teaspoon chopped fresh ginger
1 teaspoon turmeric
1 teaspoon chilli powder

1 teaspoon garam masala
1½ teaspoons cumin powder
2 teaspoons salt
1 cup of roughly chopped fresh coriander
900g (2 lb) packet of frozen peas

Heat the oil in a large saucepan, tip in the finely chopped onion, and
cook gently until soft but not browned: add the chopped ginger and
fry together for about 3 minutes. Add all the spices and the salt – Prem
had them all prepared on a plate in pretty little mounds – then stir in
the coriander leaves. Stir and cook for a minute or so until all the
flavours burst out and scent the air. Pour in the frozen peas, mix well
with all the other ingredients and simmer with the lid on the pan until
the peas are tender, about 6 minutes. Give them the odd stir now and
then. I can't tell you how good they are cooked like this.

A receipt of the señor which cooked itself at the goodness of God

I can't resist the title of this Mexican recipe for delicious little potato croquettes (culled from my nephew-in-law's mother, I think).

S E R V E S 8

8 large potatoes

salt

4 eggs

1 small onion

1 large clove of garlic

1 large tomato

100g (4 oz) seedless raisins

12 olives, stoned

12 peeled almonds

lard

225g (8 oz) minced pork

120ml (4 fluid oz) medium sherry

plain flour

Cook the potatoes in boiling, salted water. When cooked, peel them and mash with one beaten egg.

To prepare a hash, chop the onion, garlic, tomato, raisins, olives and almonds. Mix them together in a bowl and season with a little salt. Melt some lard in a pan and fry the minced pork, together with the hash mixture. Add the sherry and cook until the ingredients are fairly dry.

Prepare two bowls: one with some plain flour; and one with the remaining three beaten eggs. Press spoonfuls of the mashed potato into rounds on a board, fill them with spoonfuls of the hash and roll them into croquettes. Roll in the plain flour and dip into the beaten egg. Then fry in a little lard until nicely browned all over.

Prune sauce

There is a very good prune sauce they serve in Italy to go with pork or ham, much stronger than our dear old apple sauce, with a very zingy taste that cuts a rather fatty roast pork and crackling most enhancingly. Once made it seems to last for ages in a screwtop jar kept in the refrigerator.

SERVES 8—10

40 prunes
1 onion
100g (4 oz) prosciutto crudo (or raw gammon)
100g (4 oz) unsalted butter
2 wine glasses red wine vinegar

bay leaf
sprig of thyme
salt and pepper
water
Worcestershire sauce

Either buy stoned prunes or soak them overnight, then stone them yourself. Chop the onion and the prosciutto fairly fine and melt them in the butter. Cook until soft but not browning. Add the vinegar, turn up the heat and reduce liquid by half. Stir in the prunes, bay leaf and thyme; season judiciously. Pour in enough water to just cover the prunes. Put a lid on and simmer very slowly for two hours. When cooked and cooled a bit, blend or process into a smooth paste with a dash of Worcestershire sauce.

Winter Desserts

Whisky galore

**The beautiful Veronica Hodges, who is an extremely good egg and runs
Life for the Unborn Child, gave me the most disgusting-sounding receipt for a
pudding, which in fact turned out rather delicious. It came from a rabbi,
which should tell us something.**

SERVES 6—8

1 heaped teaspoon cocoa
1 heaped teaspoon instant coffee
1 packet gelatine (11g/0.4 oz)
175ml (6 fluid oz) boiling water

1 tin of condensed milk (385g/13½ oz)
1 tin of evaporated milk (400g/14–15 oz)
1 tumbler whisky (300ml/6–8 fluid oz)

You could use brandy or rum for this if you prefer, and I find a good
sprinkling of freshly ground coffee over the finished jelly gives a
certain oomph and texture to the wobbly whole. Mix the cocoa,
instant coffee and gelatine together then dissolve completely with the
boiling water. Combine the two tins of milk, stir in the whisky and
the gelatine mixture. Pour into a mould and leave to set in the refrigerator. Turn out when ready and serve with a crunchy sweet biscuit:
brandy snaps would be excellent I should think.

Bananas as I arrange them for guests of the last minute

A mixture of bananas, honey, cream and tequila – what could be simpler or more delicious?

SERVES 4

6 ripe bananas, peeled and sliced
juice of 1 lemon
3 tablespoons runny honey

2 tablespoons thick cream
2 tablespoons tequila or brandy

Beat the bananas to a froth. Then add the remaining ingredients, one at a time, beating after each addition. Pour into individual glasses, chill thoroughly and serve.

149

Yoghurt, cheese and honey mould

For a cleansing and fresh-tasting pudding after the rigours of suet and pastry, you might try this mould.

SERVES 8

175g (6 oz) curd cheese
750g (1 ½ lb) Greek yoghurt (Total or the like)

1 ½ teaspoons finely grated lemon rind
4 tablespoons of the best clear honey

Mix the curd cheese, yoghurt and lemon rind in a large bowl, beating until quite smooth. Place a clean tea-towel or a layer of cheesecloth over a large sieve or colander. Put the cheese mixture in the middle and let it drain into the mixing bowl for 4 hours in some cool place. Transfer into another bowl, add the honey and mix well. Line your mould or dish with dampened cheesecloth and press in the mixture. Level and leave to settle in the refrigerator for 1 ½ hours. Turn out onto a dainty dish and surround with a delicious sauce like sieved raspberries.

Suffolk frozen lemon pudding

**Now here is a nice tart lemon pudding to keep up your sleeve,
or in the freezer when your palates are jaded from too much mincemeat.
It comes from my esteemed Michael Lambton's mother.**

SERVES 8

175g (6 oz) digestive biscuits
oil
a 900g (2 lb) bread tin
3 eggs

100g (4 oz) caster sugar
2 large lemons
300ml (½ pint) double cream

Crush the digestive biscuits in a plastic bag with a rolling-pin. Oil the bread tin. Shake half the biscuit crumbs into the tin, coating the sides and the bottom. Separate the eggs. Combine the yolks with the sugar, the grated rind and juice of the two lemons. Beat until pale and creamy. Whip the cream until it forms soft peaks. Whip the egg whites stiffly. Fold both into the lemon mixture and pour into a 900g (2 lb) bread tin. Cover the top with the remaining biscuit crumbs. Cover with cling-film and foil. Freeze as long as you like. When serving, turn it out and cut into slices.

Index

potatoes
	with black olives 42
	croquettes 146
	puréed basil 70
	rosti 143–4
	Ruspoli 72
poulet béarnais 140–1
Prem's peas 145
Prince, Thane 87
Prosper, Saint 65
prune sauce 147
pudding, toffee 45
pumpkin, baked with Brazilian chopped
	beef 134
pumpkin cheesecake 113–14
pumpkin soup 89–90
puréed basil potatoes 70

rabbit
	lapin aux pruneaux 132–3
	wild, casseroled with cream and
	tarragon 100
ragout of lamb 27–8
receipt of the señor which cooked itself at
	the goodness of God 146
red fruits, lemon syllabub with 77
red pepper sauce, watercress mousse
	with 91
red wine, eggs poached in 93
redcurrent syrup 80
rémoulade, céleri 112
Ribollita, La 19–20
ricotta and beetroot salad 73
risotto, ruby red 128
rosti 143–4
ruby red risotto 128

salmon
	cardamom steamed, on bean salad
		64
	smoked, and asparagus, tarts 21–2
scallop and spinach dainties 55
Schultz, Bob 75
Scottish nettle pudding 39–40
sea bass with black olives 34
Slindon, Sussex 89
smoked salmon and asparagus tarts 21–2
smothered chicken breasts 131
soft meringues with egg custard 81–2
soufflés
	courgette 61–2
	goat's cheese 129
	mushroom 51-2
soup, chilled tomato with frozen extra
	virgin olive oil 22
Southern Italian fried chicken 107–8
spiced chicken 58
spinach and egg pie with pancetta 103–4
spinach and potato timbales 74
St George's day 30
St Valentine's day 126, 128
steak and kidney pudding 136–7
strawberry and amaretti terrine 76–7
sudden death pudding 115
Suffolk frozen lemon pudding 151
sweetbreads 101–2
syllabub, lemon, with red fruits 77

toffee pudding 45
tomato aspic ring 54
tomato soup, chilled, with frozen extra
	virgin olive oil 22
tomatoes, roast 110

Other cookery books from Headline:

Cooking for Friends Raymond Blanc
A Blanc Christmas Raymond Blanc
Modern Bistrot Cookery Antony Worrall Thompson
30-Minute Menus Antony Worrall Thompson
Vegetarian Baby and Child Petra Jackson
A Taste of Africa Dorinda Hafner
The Pudding Club Book Keith and Jean Turner
Fast Fab Food Richard Cawley